Rationales of Ownership

RATIONALES OF OWNERSHIP

Transactions and Claims to Ownership in Contemporary
Papua New Guinea

Edited by

Lawrence Kalinoe and James Leach

Sean Kingston Publishing
www.seankingston.co.uk
Wantage

First published in 2004 by

Sean Kingston Publishing
www.seankingston.co.uk
Wantage

British Library Cataloguing in Publication Data
A catalogue record for this book is available from the British Library.

Printed by Lightning Source

ISBN 0-9545572-0-4 hardback

ISBN 0-9545572-1-2 paperback

Contents

Contributors

Tony Crook is Lecturer in Social Anthropology at the University of St. Andrews.

Melissa Demian is Assistant Professor of Anthropology at Bard College.

Eric Hirsch is Senior Lecturer in the Department of Human Sciences, Brunel University and PTC Principle Investigator.

Lawrence Kalinoe is Dean of the Law School at the University of Papua New Guinea and practices law with Harricknen Lawyers, Port Moresby.

James Leach is Research Fellow, King's College and Associate Lecturer, Department of Social Anthropology, University of Cambridge.

Stuart Kirsch is Assistant Professor at the University of Michigan.

Marilyn Strathern is William Wyse Professor of Social Anthropology, University of Cambridge and PTC Principle Investigator.

Editors' Note

PROPERTY, TRANSACTIONS AND CREATIONS: NEW ECONOMIC RELATIONS IN THE PACIFIC (PTC) was an ESRC funded joint project between Cambridge and Brunel Universities in the U.K. The editors and authors gratefully acknowledge the financial support of the Economic and Social Research Council. James Leach gratefully acknowledges the support of the Leverhulme Trust and the Newton Trust during the preparation of the manuscript.

The idea for this volume came about during one of the workshops held by members of the PTC research group. As the instigator, James Leach thanks them sincerely for their willingness to participate at short notice, and for their work and input towards the project itself, which is the unseen background to the volume. We know that each of the authors in this book feels grateful to the other members of the project for their inspiration, for sharing their time and ideas, and for the hard work they have put in. Two other members of PTC, Karen Sykes and Andy Holding, have contributed to our thinking and the same thanks extends to them. Karen co-edited a companion volume, published in 2001, entitled *Culture and Cultural Property in the New Guinea Islands Region*, UBSPD: New Delhi. Adam Reed has maintained an interest in PTC matters, and been a regular contributor to our discussions for which we are all grateful.

We have benefited from collaboration with scholars in Papua New Guinea who include Colin Filer, Linus digim'Rina, Sakarepe Kamene, Don Niles and Jacob Simet. PTC co-ordinated existing anthropological data and fresh field studies. Each author here was responsible for a component of the project, in collaboration with the particular communities named in the chapters. The names of these communities also carry an acknowledgement of their input.

Eric Hirsch and Marilyn Strathern have organised the project overall. Eric Hirsch has offered guidance and insight, while Marilyn Strathern's skill and industry has been inspirational to us all throughout. Fleur Rodgers assisted at very short notice with the preparation of the manuscript, and our thanks also go to Lois Baduk at UPNG for her assistance in this regard.

Lawrence Kalinoe and James Leach, June 1999

We have decided to re-issue this volume only two years after its initial publication. This is because the initial print run, organised by the Law Faculty Publication Unit at the University of Papua New Guinea, sold out rapidly, and was mainly sold within that country. The interest in the volume was initially among lawyers and legislators who had responsibility at that time for considering the requirement to introduce Intellectual Property legislation at the bidding of the World Trade Organisation. However, those of us who teach anthropology outside Papua New Guinea have also found the studies contained herein extremely valuable for introducing students to contemporary issues of ownership and resource extraction in Melanesia. It has not only proved very popular in courses about the contemporary Pacific, but also in courses on kinship and exchange, political economy, and ownership. The re-issue is intended to make it available to a wider anthropological readership, as well as rectifying a couple of oversights in the original. We are most grateful to Sean Kingston for working with us.

James Leach, Cambridge, 15 December 2003

Preface

Rationales

This volume contains detailed ethnographic case studies from contemporary Papua New Guinea (PNG). These case studies take as their focus the documentation of particular claims to ownership. In line with the aims of the project from which this book arises (Property Transactions and Creations: New Economic Forms in the Pacific, [PTC]), the detailed cases do not attempt to be representative of the wide diversity of situations in contemporary PNG (as in a survey), but rather to be exemplary. That is, because of the depth of their ethnographic observation, they allow comparative work (for example into resource ownership) to follow from, rather than precede, the data on ownership contained therein. The book is intended as a resource for those interested in the way claims to ownership are made in particular instances. Certain operating principles whereby transactions make explicit claims to creative input of various kinds are drawn from developed understandings of actual situations.

We make two rationales of our own explicit from the outset. Firstly, the chapters are connected by their focus on ownership, not their conclusions regarding it. This makes the studies contained here concrete examples of the ways relationships and connections are mobilised in the support of claims. We aim to understand which claims are admissible, why they are, which claims have effect and which do not, in specific instances. Each case enables the authors to highlight the specific rationales of ownership in a contemporary location.

Secondly, we take the claims themselves, rather than the objects claimed, as the significant and interesting object of our study. This means attention to the transactions in which such claims are embedded. Presuming transactions as our starting point rather than resources allows freedom to describe in detail how specific transactions, and peoples' concerns within them, generate the possibilities for what may be claimed. Resources, or things claimed, are open categories in this work, to be defined situationally through attention to the ethnographic detail of transactions themselves.

The *aim* of the book is to meet the need for detailed ethnographic description of specific images and idioms of ownership in contemporary PNG. There are a number of audiences for such a work at this time, including PNG legal scholars who look to ethnographic work in defining what is admissible as customary law, a wider Papua New Guinean readership who look for documentation of different and emerging perspectives on ownership, resources and customs from different parts of the country, and anthropologists and sociologists who are interested in development, contemporary tenure, exchange and legal issues. The book may also find an arena in the reinvigorated debate on property and its alternatives. Finally, there may well be an audience, both within and beyond PNG, among those interested in the protection of what falls broadly under the heading of Intellectual Property. This is a rapidly growing area of interest among lawyers, indigenous people, NGOs and social commentators. The case studies in this book aim to tease out the complex connections between creations, persons, resources and 'culture'/*kastom* as they appear in claims over tangible and intangible items.

The *origin* of the volume is in the PTC project. This project aimed to produce knowledge of the social relations in which ownership claims are made. Taking off from a Melanesian propensity to deploy 'things' as signifiers for persons, we examine the way in which resources of various kinds are embedded in social relationships. We ask, what kind of relationship creates value? How do people mobilise relationships to connect with perceived value? How different do these creations look in the different contexts of contemporary PNG? Are there appropriate concepts in the language of law and development to describe knowledge, its value, loss, alternative modes of boundary construction, processes of value creation, belonging and so forth? In asking such questions, we aim to throw light on people's expectations and behaviour, and also on new social forms as they emerge to deal with new contingencies.

Resources themselves will be defined through ethnographic explication. Anthropologists can contribute here, as their focus on actual relationships and ethnographically generated understandings *start* from the connections and interests people relate in making claims. Conceptual clarification is in fact a resource of a kind, and one anthropologists are in a position to provide for others. This volume attempts to make some of that resource accessible.

James Leach

1

Introduction
Rationales of Ownership

Marilyn Strathern

The makers of the Papua New Guinea Constitution put a remarkable instrument into place when they determined that the underlying law of the new country was to be both English common law (as it existed at the time of Independence) and customary law.[1] Both are built up through precedent; neither have blanket applicability. Where conflict arises, they are subordinate to national laws on the statute book and to principles enshrined in the Constitution.[2] In the case of customary law, this leads to an outcome as significant at the beginning of a new century of international agreements as it was important at the beginning of Papua New Guinea's history as an independent state.

The outcome sounds obvious: customary law enacts a presumption of diversity. Rather than customary law being incorporated through a set of generalised axioms about traditional practices and expectations implying some kind of consensus, it is left as an open and uncodified field. It is up to the litigants and judges in each individual case to plead and determine the relevance of specific customary practices to the case in hand. As a consequence, however regional or local their occurrence, no customary practice is too 'small' for consideration; if it can be taken as a set of facts relevant to the case, then it carries the weight of law. This conserves the diversity of local practices without legislators having to draw up a national schedule or reducing the practices to the lowest common denominator in order to achieve consistency across the country – neither possible in practical terms, nor for that matter desirable. There are two general implications here, for which this book offers some interesting documentation. The first can be stated succinctly; the second develops some of the non-obvious yet significant features of the kinds of diversity at stake, and will require some elaboration.

First, someone not familiar with the resonances of 'custom' (*kastom*)[3] in modern Melanesia might imagine that customary law is about nostalgia for a remote past. This could not be further from the truth: for all its different connotations in various places across Papua New Guinea and the Melanesian islands, 'custom' consists of contemporary practices, and they are practices which draw on tradition insofar as tradition is part of the present. I take my cue here from Lawrence Kalinoe's (1999: 35) observation that custom in PNG has always been 'fluid, flexible and responsive to social change', and with this comes the capacity to absorb new elements. It is as important as it ever was that it remains uncodified. Here it is important too that the protocols for determining the relevance of 'customary law' refer above all to *practice*, and thus to rules only insofar as they are made evident through current practice. This book brings together contemporary case studies which show practices, so to speak, in action. They focus on one area in which the law has an interest, namely the ownership of tangible and intangible resources; they leave to one side the question of property, that is, whether these practices are in the mode of property ownership.[4]

Second, there is far more to Papua New Guinea's customary law than the preservation of idiosyncratic cultural values which enable local groups to carry on their traditions. It draws attention to the *procedures* through which people work out their relationships to one another, whether in matters of property or whatever, and whether these consist of conflict and dispute or other social processes. So here 'custom' covers a diversity in procedure. And these diverse procedures reveal a singular inadequacy in what we might call outsider understandings of local traditions – an inadequacy which becomes of more than local or national moment when such understandings are enshrined in international protocols. What is the international context? The question is a good starting point for elaborating the nature of this inadequacy, and what else we hope that this book will do.

The reference to codification, however, raises a preliminary point on which we should be explicit. Ethnography of the kind encountered in these chapters is not just a mode of documentation; it is also a means of explanation and analysis.[5] In other words, it does not pretend to a codification of 'customs', a danger which the PNG Law Reform Commission pointed out a long time ago. On the one hand it is an interpretation of them, and here serves as a salutary reminder that customary practices are always interpreted from particular vantage points; on the other hand, by putting particular practices into larger social and cultural contexts, good ethnography provides both the tools and the data by which such interpretations can be evaluated.

International assumptions about 'indigenous' peoples

From a present-day vantage point we could almost say that what was an issue in the early struggle to give a place to customary law was Papua New Guinea's 'ownership' of customary practices.

An eventuality not foreseen by the law-makers of the 1970s is the extent to which 'custom' and 'tradition' have since become part of an international language linking 'indigenous peoples' across the world in defence of their cultural heritage.[6] Key here has been the role which the United Nations has played, for example with its Working Group on Indigenous Populations (chaired by Erica-Irene Daes), and what has been nothing less than a world movement by those who refer to themselves as indigenous peoples – leading to and, even more widely, leading from the 1992 Biodiversity Convention. This movement has been energised by the perception that the resources of the developing world, in which technologically developed countries have an interest, are not just tangible (timber, minerals) but also intangible (such as 'indigenous knowledge'), and that these intangible resources include what people perceive to be of great value to themselves, namely culture or heritage. Where this is regarded as eroded or debased, culture starts taking on the characteristics of a resource itself, something of value to be claimed or preserved. On the 50th anniversary of the Universal Declaration of Human Rights, the United Nations' document on the *Protection of the Heritage of Indigenous People* (Daes 1997) fuses these separate elements as a matter of the 'cultural and intellectual property rights of indigenous people'. Cutting right across all this activity has been an alliance, beginning with Western industrial nations (through the World Trade Organisation), set up to promote a highly specific and legally binding world agreement on intellectual property rights. Here the idea is to extend internationally recognised copyright and patent law in order to protect individual rights to technological inventions. In PNG, the imminent legislation has fed into, and served to raise, people's consciousness of 'cultural property' protection (Kalinoe and Simet 1999).

The point to be made about diversity of social procedures recognised by PNG customary law is this. What we may refer to as the international community concerned with indigenous rights has put in a decade of hard and detailed work on the nature of indigenous cultures. To keep with the formulations so well expressed in the *Protection of Heritage* document, it is argued that many of the concepts of Western law are hardly applicable – notably 'property' with its connotations of individual and exclusive possession. For example: 'Heritage is, ordinarily, a communal right and is associated with a family, clan, tribe or other kinship group' (Daes 1997: iii). Yet the notion of 'communal rights' falls far short of the social realities of Papua New Guinean ideas about the interests of groups such as clans or tribes. The kinds of social procedures to which people resort show a dovetailing of individual and collective expectations socially richer and more complex than 'communal' suggests.

Commenting on the artificial distinction between cultural and intellectual property, Daes (1997:3) amplifies as follows:

> Indigenous peoples regard all products of the human mind and heart as interrelated, and as flowing from the same source: the relationships between the people and their land, their kinship with the other living creatures that share the land, and with the spirit world. ... [For example] it is inconceivable that a song, or any other element of the people's collective identity, could be alienated permanently or completely.

We would not necessarily want to quarrel with the *cultural* interpretation here, which captures the interrelatedness and holistic nature of cultural life[7]; but it is an inadequate description of *social* life.

Generalising for all 'indigenous peoples' can be understood as signalling the gravity and ubiquity of the issues. Yet it would be a great mistake to overlook the way in which, in Papua New Guinea, the flow of 'life' is channelled through *specific* persons and thus 'transacted' between them. Primarily, life and resources are owed to others as they owe it in turn. These others may be one's own ancestors – or they may literally be 'others', bush spirits or place spirits, or members of different groups. And very often what is owed has to be paid for. Against the flow of benefits, just as they do for harms, go payments in some form or other. In this way intangible benefits (well-being, renown) are rendered tangible (the wealth or sacrifice that is given in return).[9] Such transactions have to be between identifiable – named, individual – persons or groups in order to work.

The point is that in the PNG context the flow of payment *releases* the flow of life. The release is conditioned by appropriate relationships being in place; it is the payments which ensure that the flow continues.[9] If we call these 'transactions' it is to point to interactions focused on the relationships thereby sustained between the parties, rather than to the narrower Euro-American sense of an exchange of economic values which closes off relations. In the PNG context, furthermore, the circulation of 'rights' over intangibles (wealth, magic) is often bound up with 'rights' over performance (exchange, ritual).[10] Indeed, rather than talking of rights adhering to individual persons one might wish to talk of obligations adhering to relationships, so that what falls on the individual are the *debts* that he or she owes to others.[11] People transact with one another in the discharging of these debts. At the same time, transactions tend to set up their own cycles of debts, whether or not they also cancel out or create debts in other spheres of social life. Not all transactions are set within pre-existing relationships: short cycles limited to one transaction start taking on the appearance of commodity trade; it is also possible to innovate and branch out into new relationships that did not exist before. In general, however, there is an incentive to 'create' relationships – whether old relations reactivated or new ones with their future ahead of them.[12]

The concept of 'relations' is used here in a sense which is neutral as to emotional tenor or affect[13]: they do much more than just 'link' people. On the contrary they are equally well thought of as 'dividing' them. Social relations set up distinctions between persons by the very fact of the roles they take up in respect of one another – a child's maternal kin are differentiated from its paternal kin; elders and juniors occupy different positions in the transmission of knowledge; some people take it on themselves to speak for the rest, and so forth. It follows that acting out relationships may be as much about people separating themselves from another as they are about looking after one another. Indeed they may come to combine interests which are manifested in violence or dispute.

In short, social life works through distinctions which are also relationships. Whether we are talking of groups or of persons, this is abundantly evident in the ethnographic record from PNG. Distinctions (as between different clans) are also relationships (clans are linked to one another, through marriage or other forms of alliance), in the same way as persons are never known by one identity alone but always combine in themselves multiple origins. It is along these relationships that rights flow. For whether one is talking of rights to tangible or intangible resources, it is often the case that someone 'owns' something *by virtue of* it having come from another, socially distinct, person, and thus from somewhere else; if they can trace a connection or recite a name then that relationship is part of what 'ownership' means. A diversity of procedures, as customary law allows, reflects an intrinsic interest in what we could call relational or social diversity. There is much to be learnt from looking at such procedures.

If one were thinking of 'cultural property' as a kind of communal right, for example, one would have to invent an individual and bounded body which could be the bearer of this right, such as 'the Hagen people'. This would be a new social entity, defined by the rights which it now has in its perceived common heritage, and there is nothing wrong with that. As we shall see, new social entities come into being all the time. But the kinds of rights people otherwise regard as customary are rarely monolithic in this way. Bodies, we might say, are not bounded. Certainly kinsfolk never relate to one another along one path alone – they occupy different social positions depending on what is the object of interest between them. This is as true within the societies of PNG as between them. (For example: A father and son in one society may be united as consanguines, divided as members of different moieties; in another, they may be united as clan members and divided by their respective maternal kin.) The point is that *the claims* which people make over resources, assets, 'property' of all kinds, *will also be united and divided*, or in the language of property we could say they may be simultaneously exclusive and non-exclusive. (For example: A son holds his father's ritual knowledge in trust before it passes to the father's matrilineal heir: this means that the heir acquires an exclusive right, an identity with his ancestor, since only he can benefit from the magic, yet its former custodian may have an interest in how he (the heir) deploys it and may indeed have to be paid for keeping it in the meanwhile. A gardener gives his maternal cousins use-rights to his clan land: the land may be owned exclusively by the clan, as part of its identity, but that does not prevent an individual person from sharing its benefits with cousins from another clan.) Indeed, rights may be asserted which rest on being able to activate relationships and conduct transactions rather than on any claim to a common identity at all. ('Hagen' people wanting to mount a festival could actually wish to display their relationships with non-Hageners by pointing to the outside – foreign, exogenous – sources from they have purchased the rights to perform a piece of ritual. Value would come from their acting out that relationship.)

We may be able to adapt the legal terminology of multiple ownership here (e.g. to refer to joint interests rather than common interests). However the contributors to this book feel that there is preliminary work to be done, namely to lay out ways in which multiple interests are worked out in practice.[14] In most of the cases presented here, transactions of one kind or another, including negotiations in the wake of disputes, make people's presumptions and expectations evident. The cases largely follow anthropological methods, drawing on materials from contexts understood more widely (ethnographically). What renders ownership multiple, divided between persons, most importantly includes the kinds of rationales or explanations which people offer for why they are pursuing a particular claim.

Against some of the global assumptions made about the interests of ''indigenous' peoples, customary law in Papua New Guinea facilitates expressions of ownership which have to take relationships into account – and the transactions which ensue. We can think of these as having two sides, or a dual nature. On the one hand lie claims made in the name of groups or persons with their own histories and identities; on the other hand lie the flow of exchanges between them which guarantees that what is of value circulates – and continues in turn to receive the value which circulation confers.[15] Drawing parallels between human and plant communities, Swanson (1995) argues for the recognition of social and conceptual, as well as biological, diversity. We hope to make evident the value which many people in Papua New Guinea give to diversity in their management of relationships.

Assumptions behind the approach of this book

This is a brief amplification of some of the pointers set out by James Leach in the Preface.

Questions about ownership frequently arise from the need to analyse rights to resources. However, indigenous institutions, including exchange systems, may create a situation in which interests in resources run alongside interests *in persons*. The basis of such interests may be relationships of diverse kinds – kinship, partnership, political alliance – but what is the basis of the claims? Sometimes these may look like the consequences of contract, holding people to former promises, but at other times they may look like the consequences of ownership, where personal knowledge or personal ties validate a particular claim to take care of or exploit or bestow or dispose of the entity in question. The rights which ownership affords will depend to some degree on how the entity has been acquired. Valuables intended to be in constant circulation compel the recipient to pass them on, whereas heirlooms may have to be hidden away until the moment of transmission to the next generation arises.

Focusing on resources[16] makes sense when the 'things' in question are tangible assets (timber, water, minerals): it enables one to describe the relations between persons which establish the ownership of 'rights' to those resources. This helps one understand how proprietary claims arise. It is likely to produce information of immediate relevance to those concerned with the policy and with the administrative effects of resource exploitation. However, if one enlarges the field to include intellectual resources which may be intangible (knowledge, *kastom* practices, songs), we are dealing with entities which only acquire the properties of 'things' (they can be owned and transacted) in the course of communication between people. It may therefore make more sense to start with relations, and the way in which resources of various kinds are embodied in social relationships. This is the approach of this book.

As soon as one adopts this perspective, we see how claims are themselves embedded in the nature of transactions, that is, in the ways in which people deal with one another. This approach, to reiterate the Preface, is likely to produce information which will throw light on people's expectations and behaviour, and on their reactions to events; it will also throw light on new social mechanisms for dealing with new contingencies.

Many transactions take place within the stream of routine social activity, such as fulfilling obligations towards kin, marketing and trading, ceremonial exchange, borrowing a sawmill, obtaining political sponsorship for an event, and so forth. But they comprise the context in which conflicts of interest are played out. Reactions to resource compensation, for instance, come both from the conditions of resource extraction and from expectations derived from other areas of life about what can be negotiated. The problem is of course that the universe of 'transactions' is infinite. The value of documenting a handful of communities in detail is not to pretend to a comprehensive picture (an impossible project): it is to know a local situation well enough to be able to bring particular procedures into focus.

The chapters

Eric Hirsch (Chapter Two) starts with the creation of new social entities. Impetus comes from the possibility of remuneration, a theme running through many of the chapters (especially 4 and 8). Another recurrent theme first encountered here, is that the value of items lies in (among other things) their particular histories, and thus in knowing where they have come from, whether from one's ancestors or from somewhere else altogether. In listening to one such set of claims, the anthropologist's question was whether these would work as 'ownership' claims. The figure of Kol, who wanted to delimit the territory over which his people (Visi) had rights, stands out: the 'one man' who encompasses many men, and who encompasses the history of the land as a kind of personal knowledge. The claim he was making for everyone in Visi rested on the persuasiveness with which he could show that he himself 'knows' diverse locations within the area. Combined with the knowledge is the claim that he is responsible for these places, 'looks after' them. However, knowledge is not just part of a person but part of a relationship (one only knows what comes from another person), and this has consequences for who can claim to have 'looked after' something and thereby become assimilated to its origins. The limits of 'knowledge' are the limits of certain fields of relations. At the same time, it is possible to acquire land through 'purchase'. If Kol is trying to persuade others of his new vision for Visi, he himself seems to have been 'persuaded' by rumours of the mine and by the vision of the mining extension with its boundaries.

In Chapter Three, Melissa Demian shifts our attention to local dispute settlement, where we see a combination in action: the manner in which, routinely combining government 'law' with local practices (as was intended), village courts strive for new combinations between custom and money. This is evident in the handling of the abuse of a woman, where the ruling adopted local shaming procedures. People make clear separations or distinctions in the types of relationships at issue in disputes, and these become distinctions in the kind of outcome that is sought and thus in the type of forum to which people take their cases. For instance, compensation presupposes that people are separated from one another, and is well suited to 'straightening' affinal relations. It thus emerges as a tool which can be used in sorting out injuries done to persons (they are already separated from one another by the injury), in a way that is not possible where such separation is not presupposed (as in the land case discussed). In short, alleged damage (to persons and personal property) is treated differently from conflicting claims (over land). In both cases there may be contest over liability and so forth, but in the former there is no conflict of claim, only a need for restitution; while in the latter there is no immediate ground for restitution, only a conflict of claim. Even when resources are at stake, questions of 'ownership' may be overshadowed by other considerations.

James Leach (Chapter Four) shows how cases are nested in cases: nothing is ever completed. Land becomes an object of interest when it can yield products – but while the two disputes on which he reports are stimulated by 'development' prospects (the building of the road, his purchase of the drum), he makes a more general argument for seeing the products of Nekgini land as the place where 'value' lies. The point here is that the products do not reflect the value of the ground as such, but refer to the work which went into their production. Work is embedded in product not in a commodity sense (e.g. a monetary evaluation of labour value / exchange value) but in terms of the relationships summoned to carry it out. It 'belongs' to those who participated in its creation. If value is ultimately put on that joint work then it is a value being put onto the capacity to mobilise relationships: the ultimate productive resource is people's relations with one another. This means, in turn, that there can be no simple equation of groups with land, and indeed in this part of PNG it may be misleading to talk of land-owning 'clans' at all – a salutary lesson in the context of assumptions about groups with boundaries (see Chapter Two). Groups are not isolated entities, but work in relationship with others; legitimate connections to land by one set of people need not be at the expense of others.

Lawrence Kalinoe (Chapter Five) addresses the extent to which the ownership of rights of various kinds in land amounts to a property interest, legally understood. He distinguishes various kinds of claims in customary practices, as they correspond to title, possession, trusteeship, beneficial ownership and so forth – of which (full) 'ownership' is one. Taking as his starting point the fact that in PNG claims rest on demonstrable relationships, as through genealogies, he shows that these various modes of ownership correspond to distinctive dimensions in the relations people have with one another. In the case he takes up we see a judge converting 'possession' into 'ownership'. The issue is that the judge is concerned with people's relation to the land, and the successful clan is seen to have the land (as a 'thing') in its possession. This ignores the indigenous principle that rights over things are not just rights exercised in respect of persons but derive from persons, and thereby discounts the nature of the tie between original owners and subsequent occupiers. The case is discussed in the context of common law debates over possession and his own studies of water resources (riparian land), in which ownership is clearly distinguished from usufructuary right. To owners or users alike, much of the value of the land (as in Chapter Four) is in what it produces. But the rationales behind their claims differ.

If transactions are of interest in thinking about ownership claims, in Chapter Six Stuart Kirsch considers the nature of the social networks mobilised through such events. He follows the way in which people on Lihir negotiate their relations with the Lihir gold mine company through compensation claims for what they perceive as environmental damage. Claims are formulated by making networks evident and explicit. The chain of events or chain of relationships which constitutes the network can help build up the rationale for demonstrating both the company's liability and the extent of the injury. In the course of doing so, Lihirians also demonstrate how they bring a wider world into their own purview. What is interesting about the examples is the contrast they offer to those Western or Euro-American strategies of ownership where people often press for rights on the basis of exclusion rather than inclusion. Strategy is the key word here, however, because the length of the network also depends on the nature of the claim in hand, and the chapter shows situations in which people summon short as well as lengthy configurations.

In Chapter Seven, Tony Crook takes up the 'combination' of customary and common law as itself an example of many combined outcomes, in this case the way one might mesh together PNG ideas of ownership and international expectations about Intellectual Property Rights (IPR). He thus borrows an analogy from Angkaiyakmin (rationales are invariably found in combination, whether or not the parties are equals) through which to think about the relationship between 'WTO' and 'PNG'. His notion of combination comes from understanding the way Min people put narratives together, as they do persons. Each relationship is a combination of sources (such as residence and substance, the 'two sides' of paternal and maternal kin), and if people trace their claims through relationships, then they are likely to be summoning more than one rationale. Different rationales modify or restrict one another and what can be combined can be uncombined, but the logic allows even the most important knowledge (*awem*) to be transmissible between different persons. As in Chapter Two, when a man becomes identified with the source of the knowledge he holds, each person in this transaction becomes a 'part' of the other. Indeed, much of the value which this knowledge has for the receiver is that it has come from an outside source. The chapter ends with a way of imagining PNG and international interests together. The combination may be of unequals, but the logic of the 'two sides' is compelling.

Recognising the importance of customary law as an instrument in the development of 'a truly indigenous jurisprudence, or underlying law, within which common law and customary law blend into and supplement one another.' (Kalinoe 1999: 314) is to endorse a flexibility of procedure. It is not to endorse prejudice. The final chapter (Marilyn Strathern, Chapter Eight) ends with a problematic case which drew the attention of human rights activists. The plight of the woman at the centre of the Minj compensation case would be just the kind of predicament which motivated a body of women to petition parliament in 1991 – their protest was that 'Under the pretext of respecting cultural values, the female gender are being enslaved in their homes and gardens, assaulted and abused' (quoted by Jessep and Luluaki 1994: 3). This is absolutely right. However the chapter speaks to another, counterintuitive, issue: local traditions may uphold universal values. It does not follow that because something is local it is not also of much more general interest. As a domain recognised by the law but not enacted by it, customary law has enormous procedural potential here. It can give breathing space to values and interests that might otherwise be discounted or overlooked. What assistance it would have been in the other case discussed, which involved a biotechnology patent on blood cells from the Hagahai people, is a debatable point. But in its absence it seems that all kinds of rationales of ownership could be attributed to them (the Hagahai), and thus imagined on their behalf.

What this book demonstrates is that we do not have to imagine: we can find out. The people referred to in these chapters live by cultural and social practices which make them – whether for good or ill – reflect on relationships and their interdependencies; a quite separate issue is that they have been, with characteristic generosity, prepared to articulate what they think. That their rationales for ownership do not always fit into what might be imagined for them is the challenge.

Notes

1. It would have been even more remarkable had the programme of reforms on which the Law Reform Commission embarked in its early years been carried to fruition (see Narakobi 1982). I refer particularly to the draft legislation known as *The Underlying Law Bill 1977* which was intended to give customary law a greater role in the underlying law (Law Reform Commission 1977).

2. And in the case of customary law to 'general principles of humanity'. However, custom prevails over common law.

3. *Kastom* means much more than the English term conveys, varies across the regions of Papua New Guinea and Melanesia, and has significant local connotations. See for example the documentation carried out by the Vanuatu Cultural Centre (Bolton 1999).

4. An important aspect of this has been treated extensively by one of us (Kalinoe) elsewhere. In a detailed critique of the notion of 'communal property' he expounds the importance of clans and tribal groups as corporate groups holding property interests in various resources. By virtue of their membership, individual members of these groups acquire usufructuary rights, but do not individually have a property claim as such; that is vested in common in the group as a whole (1999: 279–300). He makes two important points. (1) It is erroneous to imagine that common rights mean anybody or everybody has access (1999: 300); PNG groups may assert exclusive interests,

which is what enables one to talk of property. (2) Similarly, it is not sufficient to make a vague gesture towards 'customary water rights', as is found, for instance, in the statute law on water management; it is possible, through detailed investigation, to be quite specific about the disposition of those rights among persons.

5. To take one example from the anthropological literature: whether events are described as gift exchanges or as trade in commodities is in part a *theoretical* matter. That is, it is not possible to tell from just looking at it whether an item is a 'gift' or a 'commodity': the writer will use the term that comes from his or her theoretical model of the working of society as a whole. Disagreements among anthropologists in this field (to do with relations of ownership) have been a fruitful source of debate precisely because the issues are significant for understanding the nature of social relations, and have not been closed off or already decided. It is 'ethnography' which in the first place raises questions for discussion.

6. Indigenous knowledge is sometimes taken as a subset of traditional knowledge, that is, as 'the knowledge, innovations and creativity embodying the traditional lifestyles of indigenous peoples' (Shozo Uemura, Deputy Director General of the World Intellectual Property Organisation [WIPO], to the WIPO Roundtable on Intellectual Property and Traditional Knowledge, Geneva, 1999).

7. For example, a similar passage from Daes is quoted with emphatic approval by Garrity (1999: 1203) in his examination of Maori concepts of intellectual property, which makes a strong cultural case for interpreting Maori ideas in terms of a holistic and relational vision of the world .

8. Daes may be right that elsewhere this is recognised in the fact that, under appropriate circumstances, people may *share* their heritage with others (p. 3); but the term 'sharing', which perpetuates the notion of communal identity, hardly covers the kinds of transactions, or range, found in PNG. At the same time such transactions only sometimes fall within the purview of *contract,* since they are often obligatory, or take place between persons related in many ways to one another who are already bound to one another.

9. This has somewhat the spirit of early IPR patent legislation which traded the continuing flow of long term knowledge for a short term monopoly. Now, the speed of innovation and realisation of assets, measured against the relatively long time it takes for product development in high technology situations, has swung the balance away from the advantage of the long term flow to the high value of the short term monopoly.

10. A point examined, for instance, in some of the contributions to Sykes with Simet 2000.

11. The question of 'obligation' is also voiced in Sykes with Simet 2000.

12. These are not gender neutral generalisations. It is often the prerogative of men to ensure that the 'flow' is maintained (e.g. Weiner 1986); women may well have another view of the matter , as they always have (e.g. Josephides 1985). The same point may also be made with respect to 'transactions' as such, and access to the wherewithal (valuables, money) with which to be effective through exchange, asymmetries which may have a long history to them (Strathern 1972).

13. It is necessary to say this because English speakers often regard 'relations' sentimentally – as axiomatically solidary and co-operative. No such gloss is intended here.

14. See Sykes with Simet 2000. This observation is made with the modification that interests are combined, rather than serially or severally pursued, so that we may talk of the combined interest which parties have to the relationship between them. Each acts, from their own particular position, with reference to the other.

15. They may involve 'individual' claims (as in claims to usufructuary use of garden land); they may involve corporate claims (a clan seeks indemnity as a group for a homicide). But they may also involve claims set up by persons in partnership or in an exchange relationship or through a kin tie that are *neither* 'individual' *nor* 'collective'.

16. And this had been done to exemplary effect, e.g. in Filer with Sekhran 1998; Toft 1997.

2

Mining Boundaries and Local Land Narratives (*tidibe*) in the Udabe Valley, Central Province

Eric Hirsch

When was entification?

Papua New Guineans are currently experiencing, either directly or indirectly, widespread operations of resource extraction from their lands. In places throughout the country we find entities such as 'clans' or 'councils of chiefs' adopted as part of the process of people becoming 'landowners' and receiving various forms of 'compensation' or rent. Before the extensive advent of resource extraction, these entities – clans or councils of chiefs – often did not locally exist (see Filer 1997, 1998; Jorgensen n.d.a., n.d.b.; Sturzenhofecker 1994). Recently, Ernst (1999) has discussed these matters among the Onabasulu. He refers to the local adoption of 'clans' as a process of 'entification': 'the process of making "entities" or things from what have been contingent categories' (Ernst 1999: 89). Ernst suggests this is a new process, one initiated by mining companies and other resource extractors, whereby local people are required to transform themselves into (landowning) entities.

There is an important question, though, as to whether entification is 'new'? Is the process, as Ernst describes it, 'new', or rather are the circumstances in which it occurs 'new' and striking? As is well documented in much previous Melanesian ethnography (see Strathern 1988) the means by which persons render themselves into named entities is a recurrent feature of Melanesian social life. Certainly 'new' forms of entification emerged during the colonial period, when language groups became 'named', or government and mission stations established – their names becoming labels often used by local people. The usage of Fuyuge, the people discussed in this chapter, is a case in point; as is the wider linguistic/cultural area of which they form a part, Goilala (see Hallpike 1977).

My concern here is not to dispute the significance of entification – its indigenous and analytical significance is beyond doubt. Rather it is to suggest that entification is not a new development or emergent form in itself, but an intermittent local process whereby persons present themselves as visible and powerful. Of course the persons as much as the circumstances for them to act in these ways are subject to historical transformation. Ernst captures one such moment in connection with current local resource extraction. This chapter engages with an analogous historical transformation among the Fuyuge, Central Province.[1]

Ononge on Visi land

During the mid 1980s I lived in the Udabe Valley of the Fuyuge. Most of my time there I was resident among the c.450 people of Visi, a 'home' on the upper, western side of the Udabe. Several times during my residence I was told, in what seemed to be a less than critical manner, that Ononge[2] (northern neighbours of Visi) lived on their land. This claim was accompanied by explicit or implicit reference to a narrative (*tidibe*, see below). The narrative indicated how ancestors of Visi came to move from lands further north (near the current boundary with the home of Woitape).

I first heard reference to Ononge being on Visi land two months after my arrival in the Udabe. It occurred when many from Visi travelled to the southern home of Tafade in order to collect smoked *malag* (a type of pandanus) from the local men and women. The *malag* would later be used as part of the distributions at a *gab*[3] in Visi. During the c. one week at Tafade, when Visi men and women were at a distance from their home, I recorded several matters about Visi that came up in conversations, several which at the time did not seem relevant to my then current ethnographic interests. The reference to Ononge living on Visi land was a case in point: it remained in my notebooks as an interesting claim or fact. I was told that Ononge's land was in the neighbouring Auga Valley. In many respects this appeared to be confirmed by the fact that Ononge's dialect was different to all others in the Udabe and shared many similarities with those spoken in the Auga Valley.

Sometime later during my first period of field research I was told a short *tidibe* – a narrative (figure) which is the source or origin of present circumstance. Fuyuge speak of *tidibe* as the basis of human strength and efficacious capacities. In order to clarify the sense of *tidibe* I refer to another, more elaborate example of this narrative form. In the Udabe Valley there is a *tidibe* known as Hufife and Aling, 'man' and 'woman' respectively. Hufife and Aling is not the only *tidibe* as such, but is an exemplar of this source of power. The narrative of Hufife and Aling recounts a series of their movements and incidents from the Chirima Valley in the east, through the Udabe Valley, to the Yaloge Valley in the west and beyond. What eventually occurred to Hufife and Aling is left as a question in the narrative. It is through this series of movements and incidents that Fuyuge men and women speak of their lands and their modes of conduct of having been 'laid down'[4] (cf. the notion of *dema* discussed by van Baal (1966) and further explicated by Weiner (1995)).

The brief narrative or *tidibe* I was told, after the visit to Tafade, focused on a ridge called Fasango (now referred to by the man who 'looks after' it as Taurama, see below). A version of this narrative went as follows:

He[5] was sitting down and then Fagubu (bird) went up and sat above him on the tree and he was singing. Fagubu or they call it Anele. He slept and he was listening and said, 'Ago.' He said, 'Poor Fagubu he is singing on the ginam tree at Fasango.' He broke the container of water[6]. After breaking the container he went up and cut the ropes of his hammock. He came down to Fasango.

The 'he' of the narrative is sitting down at a place near the boundary between Woitape and Visi land (near Ilimo, see below). At this place he hears the Fagubu or Anele bird. He then sleeps, and in his sleep he hears this bird again, but on a tree at Fasango in present day Visi. The voice of the bird makes him feel sad and he travels down to Fasango. The origins of those who have come to reside in Visi are, as indicated in this narrative, to be found near the boundary with Woitape: hence the claim that this is Visi land.

This *tidibe* was similar to others I was told in that its recitation accounted for the current state of affairs – whether settlement or conduct. In addition, I was told similar narratives which accounted for how a man and his subsequent descendants from across the Udabe at Kambisi had come to settle on Visi land. This man had been 'chased' away from Kambisi. As such, his descendants were 'guests' (*vas*) on Visi land and could not be chiefs (*amede*).

By 1999, the claim that Ononge were living on Visi land had come to take on a different significance. This change was entirely due to the proposed extension of the Tolukuma gold mine from the Auga Valley into the Udabe Valley, and in particular the proposed boundaries of the mining extension (see Hirsch 2001).[7] In short, the proposed boundary of the mining extension, as understood by people in the Udabe Valley, would exclude Visi from land which they claim is theirs.

An outgrowth of this change was that I was told a much expanded and elaborated narrative to account for this claim – some of which was an elaboration of the previous *tidibe* and some of which had more the character of a 'map', circumscribing Visi land. In addition, the circumstances in which this was told differed significantly from those of the mid 1980s. Whereas the earlier occasions I was told this narrative occurred in what I can only characterise as an 'exposed' manner, the narration during 1999 was all but secret and surrounded with much circumspection. This difference is both connected with the proposed boundary and the more elaborate claims disclosed in this expanded narrative.

Kol's narrative

The narrative was told to me by Kol Usi at Yuvenise, in the presence of Alphonse Hega, Kol's brother's son. I recorded it on tape and later, in Port Moresby, Alphonse and I translated it into English. Kol was particularly concerned that the names of numerous places mentioned in the narrative (rivers, ridges, pools, pythons) were not disclosed, as others may falsely claim the land through access to these names. As a result of his concern I have altered many of the names in the narrative below. What I have reproduced here is done so with Kol's assent.

In effect the narrative begins in a similar manner to the version recalled above. However, after some time its character changes. It begins to trace out the boundaries of Visi land through a detailed account of various places, their names and distinctive features, and their interconnections. The reason for this appears obvious, as Kol wants to assert the claims of Visi to this land. To have this knowledge is to have the capacity to look after the places; to have this knowledge is to be analogous to their source, their *tidibe*.

In what follows I have divided Kol's narrative into several parts in order to analytically separate what I interpret as distinctive segments. Kol spoke continuously and did not break up the narrative as indicated below. My commentary, where integrated into the narrative, is in brackets.

1. Taurama, that range coming up.[8] The ridge's name is Fasango. This place's father is from here to Ilimo. [In other words, the person who looks after this place, looks after all the land from here to Ilimo.] Mo is on this side and Ili is on the other.[9] He was staying there and then went up to Ungulutu. He was staying there. He carried the water and then he was sitting down. His name is Sima; Sima what? He was sitting down and then Fagubu (bird) went up and sat above him on the tree and he was singing. Fagubu or they call it Anele. He slept and he was listening and said, 'Ago'. He said, 'Poor Fagubu he is singing on the ginam tree at Fasango.' He broke the container of water.[10] After breaking the container he went up and cut the ropes of his hammock. He came down to Fasango.

The section of the narrative above is similar to accounts I was told years previously. Emphasis in the previous accounts, as now, was on the sadness evoked in hearing the sound of the bird's voice: the manner in which the narrative is recounted suggests that it is this evocation of sadness which 'caused' the movement to Fasango.

The narrative then returns from Fasango (Visi) to the original point of departure, but the main protagonist has now transformed. He has become an actual ancestor of two (living) Visi men, fathers of the land traced in the narrative. He encounters intruders on his land, whom he dispenses with and then departs for Visi.

2. One day he went back (to Ungulutu). An Omale man or a Kambisi man or a Woitape man?[11] Their names were Kwail and Kabog [two brothers]. Where the two rivers meet, Avan and Angul, you go up a bit, there is a place called Adibiti. Visi's swamp is called Saudigo. In that swamp there is a pandanus.[12] These two Woitape men, Kwail and Kabog, cut the pandanus. They cut the pandanus and split it. This place's father is a Visi man. His name is Bodi Wasamb. He went and saw these two splitting the pandanus and they were cracking it. They heaped some and they were breaking some. He went and saw them and said: 'Ago, what are you doing?' And they said the cuscus cut the pandanus and we are breaking it. One of them, whether Kwail or Kabog, brought the pandanus and then said that the cuscus cut the pandanus, we came and saw it and cut the rest down. Bodi Wasamb got the stick (*fude*) for splitting pandanus in the middle from one of them. I will break the pandanus and you two crack them and eat them. They got the pandanus and they were cracking. He got the fude and hit Kwail's head and hit Kabog's head. He hit one and then hit one. He left them there. There is a man named Ko Fagi living at Ononge, his grandfather's name is Somb Kum. Bodi Wasamb told Somb Kum that he killed the two men from Woitape. I killed the two men and I am going. [He told Somb Kum] you look after the Saudigo and the Kombu and Samleb. You look after them, I will go down and then check you. Yavi So and So Leo, their grandfather's name is Wasamb.

The next long section of the narrative traces, in effect, a 'map' of Visi land (see map). I speak of this as a map but this was neither Kol's, nor later, Alphonse's term. The reason why I have chosen to speak of this as a map is that it appears that Kol is *orienting* the listener to particular effect. He wants the listener to see these distant places, from the current location of its recitation (Yuvenise), as places we could find and recognise through his account. He is not describing one or two places but an entire realm. In fact, the Papua New Guinea topographic survey map (1:100000 scale, 'Wasa' sheet) later used by Alphonse to record these places did not provide enough detail for this purpose.

In describing this 'map' Kol leaves the narrative (*tidibe*) above and begins to trace a boundary around what he claims is Visi land. His account focuses

MAP OF NARRATIVE (TIDIBE)

on the details of specific places as he traverses the boundary. The names and actions of ancestors are the key features. As indicated above, Kol was very concerned that these names were not disclosed. To know the names is to know the place and thus to be able to demonstrate one's claims to that place.

At one point Kol's account connects with a well known *tidibe*, that of Hufife and Aling (see above; and see Hirsch 1987; 1994). There is another *tidibe* referred to at the end of this section, known as Kele Ken.[13] I did not encounter this *tidibe* during my previous fieldwork, but this is perhaps because its field of action was more centred in an 'Ononge' location, a locale which under contemporary circumstances has been called into question.

The narrative now returns to Ungulutu, where Bodi Wasamb returned after he travelled to Visi (Fasango). The boundary Kol traces moves from this northern location to the south, along the way indicating the western extent of Visi land; to the boundary between Visi and Kase – southern neighbours of Visi. He does not, however, take the listener 'straight' along this boundary, but precedes in several different directions which I endeavour to highlight below.

> 3. The Visi's forest went as far as Ungulutu. Their river's name is Hadad; python named Tabube. [Here Kol refers to a python (*manufe*) laid down by *tidibe*: these are men in the form of snakes. They appear to a dreaming person in the form of an old man after the person has entered a *kowas* (dangerous/sacred place).] Their [Visi's] ridge names are Suvago and Sirigode. And the other river's name is Mo. Their pandanus *hamad* name is Gobop *hamad*. [Again, a *hamad* is a form laid down by *tidibe*; this is a pandanus archetype.] It is growing opposite of Hobas Endant (Woitape). Where your grandfather Bodi planted the pandanus (*hin* and *yavu*). The name of the place is Anko. The pandanus is Simabab. Above it is an Ingima Kasi [type of vine]. The flying fox's name is Koboelas. [The grandfather referred to is that of Alphonse. It is likely, although Kol did not say it explicitly, that the names of the pandanus, flying foxes, and vines referred to here all derive from *tidibe* – as with the *hamad* above.] Where Bodi planted the pandanus, and where Jovani Gepa built his house. Before there was no pandanus there. They used to stay underneath the very thick forest vines. They would cut sticks and make the *hafale* [platform for drying pandanus] on these vines and cut wild *yavu* [pandanus] and put on *hafale* and dry it. There was no pandanus there. [Kol now takes the listener to a southern location of Visi's land by following the two rivers, Ili and Mo, to their source. He connects up this source with areas of land around Mount Tafa, to the boundary of Kase land and where their land extends. He indicates the limits of Kase land and what is the mark of Visi's.] You follow the two rivers up, Ili and Mo, and at the source of Ili it is called Idebode. Gobane or Iriban went up and joined Nengrube. It went up to Kemgode [close to Mount Tafa]. The land went at the back of Mount Tafa; went to a place called Ambomad. From Ambomad started Kase's land. Their land went as far as Eb and Alani and Yalog; went as far as Bolod. Bolod is ours [Visi]. Our *ginal* tree is growing there, named Molginal. You come up a bit and have Febeboku.

Kol has now established the northern, southern and western extensions of Visi land. The eastern limit is the Udabe River itself. Between this eastern and western boundary are forest (*mawant*) and warmer, lowland areas, subject to many years of cultivation (*halai*). Forest is continually transformed into *halai*. During this part of his narrative Kol is focused on forested areas; below he will trace a path to Visi through *halai*. In this forested area he moves his narrative between southern and northern locales. As indicated above, many of the names Kol mentions, Alphonse was unable to locate for me on a large scale topographic map.[14]

Close to village named Henang; there are some places named Kombu, on the other side, and Samleb is on this side [see above]. Just above it is Hobolili and Beganise. They are close to Miku. One of their river names is Og. Their ridge is Selanghenang. Our land is called Hadulan; you go down a bit and there is a river Hadubobo. That is the mark. From that mark you go and that is our land. Our ancestor's name is Hin Kedi. That is the forest name. The land went as far as Hemebas. [This part of the narrative focuses on a number of places indicating the boundary of Visi and Kase land and places internal to Visi land. The last named, Hemebas is indicated on the accompanying map. Here is where a significant exchange occurred with a Visi man, as Kol proceeds to signify.] Obu Oku got *esef* [bird feathers] and bought the pandanus [*yavu*]. He is looking after that forest. Basi and Migu's father is Obu Oku. Where the houses are now, the place is Seskulan, is where our ancestors made their house. A place called Fibgabi. Close to Fibgabi you have Hevikimi. Obu Oku gave the *esef*; his children are Basi and Migu and their children are Ebu, Ore and Geda Sila. They were cutting the pandanus and got the land. The Visi man's name is Hemed Kimani.

Kol then shifts the narrative to places further south again. He refers to forest belonging to the descendants of Bodi Wasamb (Yavi So and So Leo). The other forest he connects with belongs to Alphonse and himself. Again, Kol draws attention to various pythons and a dog laid down by *tidibe* and further evidence of previous occupation by Visi ancestors. He also indicates that mine exploration people had consulted him about the names of particular places.

In Yalog is a river called Hoka: on the other side, is a place called Tobo. Yavi So and So Leo's forest, and ours is in the middle of Hoka and Yalog. The python's name is Gilidon. It is staying at Botogenamb. The land came up to Besaenamb, up to Gubuem; the place called Yifhadofe. They planted the pandanus and called the place Giliem. There is a pool there, on the side of the pool you will see cordyline, that is where the ancestor's house was before. They used to stay there and hunt. Two of our pythons' names are Ho and Fatina. Yifugode is close to where they are staying. One of the river names is Bu. Our dog's name is Vangi, it is staying there. You follow Bu up and you come to a pool, nobody knows the name of this pool; exploration people asked me but I did not tell. One Kase man said Kol, that is not your forest. Kase woman heard it and told Kol. Kase woman told the Kase man it is not his. Woman said we do not own the land up there.

These last portions of this part of the narrative further draw attention to places associated with pythons laid down by *tidibe*. Kol also connects his account with other named *tidibe*, particularly that of Hufife, who along with his wife Aling, travelled across the Udabe Valley to the Yalog Valley. He refers to a rock with enhancing capacities, and finally concentrates on the boundary between Kase and Visi land, making it clear that a Kase man is living on Visi land.

This river Bu came and made a pool and the two pythons, Ho and Fatina, swim in this pool. When these two pythons [are] swimming in the pool, they would block the opening. It would start building up, they would swim and flow out and then block it again and so on. When you are close up you will hear it flowing and then stop and so on. [...] the river you come up to Kele Ken, he is a *tidibe*. He went and made a hammock and is sleeping under the waterfall – [I] do not know the name of the waterfall, it was not told by grandfather. The pool where the two pythons swim is called Olanbes. There is a cliff of stone called Henangpela. Close to this is Bibianfae. That is where Hufife slept and came to Yalog. He came and danced at Tedegendant. There is a *yal* [tree]; this is the *yal* that Hufife got for the dancing. He used the leaves and planted the branches there. The yal is called Henangyal.

You come up to Hodulomor. There is a stone called Mango – [one] rubs hands on stone to make [things] grow big, or scapes bits off [for the same purpose]. One of the ridge names is Halkol. Our ancestor's pandanus (*yavu*) is Gambagu. The land went up to Mokukum. Kase is at the back of the mountain and we are on this side. The land came as far as Hidokum. The land went to a place called Geluvala. The land came as far as Nuboem. Some Visi are on the other side and we are this side. Obu Kamine [Kase] is living on our land. Before my father Kol, Yavu and Manum, they cut the forest there and made their garden. This Nuboem is named after a ridge from Inai [Yalog].

The narrative then returns to Bodi Wasamb and what appears to be his departure for Visi. The land Bodi Wasamb is leaving is not Visi per se: Visi[15] is the name of an area connected with persons who speak the same dialect and who see themselves as distinct from their neighbours because of this common settlement and dialect. This is what Fuyuge refer to as *em* or 'home'. Among those who currently live in Visi are some, Yavi So and So Leo, whose origins can be traced to Bodi Wasamb. Kol and other Visi are connected with these origins through marriage and other relations.[16]

The names of various interlinked roads are indicated, roads which Bodi Wasamb would have followed before spotting his ridge (Fasango/Taurama) from Ononge. The roads he traverses are ones that trace movements through *halai* – particularly *halai* that are now claimed by Ononge; the entire area of Visi land is now considered. Again, his movement along these roads has its origins in the sadness evoked by hearing the sound of the Fagabu. At the end of his account Kol reiterates the limits of Visi land, separating what is Visi from what is that of Woitape and that of Pata (the Auga Valley). He is suggesting that unnamed others are making claims about the extent of Visi's claims to land. Kol is demonstrating through his knowledge of persons, Iworl Hadam etc., the extent of Visi land. The limits of Visi land are reckoned by the limits of persons: to go beyond this boundary is to encounter persons with knowledge and claims analogous to that demonstrated by Kol, but over a different, contiguous realm.

4. [From above.] Bodi Wasamb followed the river Avan, he came to Hevenhuso, he came up to Yandene, he came to Gavi, he came to Mawote, he came up to Emand, came under Keef, came up to Valas, came up to Yovans [followed ridge to Evese] he came down and went to Halandtu, went down to Lolof to Konamu went down Usin [road between Ononge and Visi]. He saw his ridge from Ononge. Ungulutu is Yavi So's forest. Some Ononge say our land went as far as Fatima to Omboli. But this is Pata's land. Yulhai their forest. Some say our land went as far as Sirivagode; our land is on this side but Woitape is on the other side. They are mixing it up. They are telling lies. Our mark is Ili and Mo. A ridge comes close to Ilimo, called Lude, it is Pata land. The man from Pata is Iworl Hadam... Himbol and Gabi. He is from Yuwai [part of Woitape]. Pata's forest. Himbol is from Woitape and Gabi is from Pata.

'Looking after' (*afomeme*)

At one point in Section 3 of the above narrative, Kol highlights a transaction which occurred. This is where Obu Oku 'purchased' the pandanus through the transaction of bird feathers, *esef*. Immediately after, Kol says that Obu Oku is 'looking after' that forest: 'Obu Oku got *esef* [bird feathers] and bought the pandanus [*yavu*]. He is looking after that forest.' It is through the transaction that a person unconnected to the land can now 'look after' it. By implication, then, all the other places Kol refers to in his account are 'looked after' by him and other Visi.

But what does he mean by 'looking after'? The forest is now 'part' of him (i.e. Obu Oku) through the transaction. He is not different from the forest (such as one would speak of a person with whom one had no relations, *an kigi* – a separate person). To look after is to know; but one knows because what one looks after is part of the person. In this manner of thinking one could ask how one could look after that which one does not 'know'? To know is to be part of persons and relations. In other words, one can only know that which derives from another person,[17] either through direct communication (being taken to see it and learning the names etc.) or through a transaction which imparts this knowledge. The fact that Kol, for instance, knows the names and details of the places in his narrative indicates that he has some relation with the land: it is through a relation with a person who knows, or previously knew, that land becomes part of the person.

To have the relation of 'knowing' or 'looking after' is to partake of the source of origin of this knowledge and persons. This is the *tidibe*: the ultimate source of that which exists. To be one that looks after, then, is to become *tidibe*-like, originary. Kol is claiming this originary status in the claims he is making about the extent of Visi land.

All the *tidibe* I have heard over the years recount a movement or journey of figures. As noted above, these are said to be the source of current arrangements and practices (e.g. death, sexual relations, animal order, etc.). Section 3 of Kol's narrative is not an explicit *tidibe*, as in the preceding sections, but it is drawing on a *tidibe*-like artifice of creating a movement by orientating the listener along a 'journey' of Visi's land boundary. Kol is claiming an originary status in these matters.

Is Kol's knowledge persuasive; is Kol asserting 'ownership'?

Kol is a great chief (*amede inoge*) of Visi, together with his elder brother Yavu. He speaks for Visi in *gab* ritual and on other 'political' occasions. He envisions himself, and others recognise him, as 'looking after' Visi. During my earlier fieldwork one young man referred to him as like a 'king'. Rumsey (2000) has recently explicated the 'I' discourse of figures such as Kol: simultaneously 'partible' – as part of other persons – and 'encompassing' – as consolidating all of these parts within one figure, through both speech and imagery. In the present instance Kol is drawing into his person all the land (persons) he claims is Visi: looking after, here, is analogous to speaking for.

The question, though, is whether Kol's knowledge and the claims he is making on the basis of this knowledge is 'persuasive'. Can his claim 'look' like 'ownership'? This final question is prompted by an interesting perspective on property and ownership proposed by Rose (1994). She writes as a lawyer and legal scholar, but her work is informed by the same kinds of problems as addressed by anthropologists and historians: how did current Western notions of property and ownership come to assume their present forms; how do such notions impinge upon our analytical concepts? Her critical work on property and ownership is premised on a seemingly unremarkable question: how do people come to be persuaded that particulars things can be owned or exist as property?

In her account, she demonstrates how people talk themselves into accepting forms of ownership; those who can talk (and act, often violently) in the most powerful and persuasive manner are those who define what property is and how it appears. One only has to consider the historical ecological account of Cronon, *Changes in the land* (1983) – about the early relations between Indians and colonists in New England – to witness the accuracy of such an argument. In short, the Indians were seen to not 'properly' occupy the land, thereby 'wasting' its wealth and potential. As a result, the white New Englanders assumed its ownership and made it appear 'properly', as individually owned property.

In general Rose (1994: 297, original emphasis) notes:

> There is an old adage, told of plain people and plain things: what you see is what you get. Property seems plain in this way too: what you see is what you get. But things are more complicated than that. With property, that nature of "things" imposes their own quite fascinating constraints. Yet even with those, *what you see* in property is what you and others have talked yourselves into about those "things"; and given some imagination, you may always talk yourself into seeing something else – with all the effects on understanding and action that a new "envisioning" may bring.

Rose's last phrase is of interest: 'a new "envisioning"'. Before things can assume the condition of being owned they must be first perceived in a specific manner. But this perception – envisioning – requires a discourse in order to render it persuasive, convincing. It would seem that the envisioning and the persuasion each imply the other.

Let us re-direct Rose's observations about property to the question of whether Ononge is on Visi's land. Kol's narrative summons a *tidibe* and takes us around a map in a *tidibe*-like manner. We are being taken to key places and along key roads whereby Kol can demonstrate that he *knows* these places; to know them is in effect to look after them. To know the names is to know the place and to know both is to establish that they are a part of the narrator. Kol's knowledge is meant to *persuade* those in a (potential) dispute that the land is Visi's (i.e. 'his' land).

Is Kol's narrative persuasive? He has certainly been 'persuaded' by rumours of the mine and by the vision of the mining extension with its boundaries. Does it look like ownership? Of course this depends on who he has to convince and how they 'see' matters. Among other Fuyuge – certainly in the case of Alphonse – Kol's claim appears very persuasive. Alphonse noted that many of the place names Ononge people routinely use are names in Visi dialect! But will others be persuaded – personnel of the mine or government agents? This is a questions which goes to the heart of this volume, to the rationales of ownership.

Conclusion: A new 'entification' of Visi?

Let us return to the opening discussion about entification. There I mentioned Ernst's (1999) analysis of the recent adoption of 'clans' among the Onabasulu as part of their strategy to 'entifiy' themselves in relation to resource extractors. An analogous process in respect to 'clans' and the 'council of chiefs' has also begun among the Fuyuge (see Filer 1997; Hirsch 2001).

However, can we also consider Kol's narrative as a innovative form of entification? I want to suggest that Kol is 'entifying' Visi in a manner not made explicit before – I certainly encountered nothing like it during my previous fieldwork. Is the manner in which Kol is rendering Visi a 'clearly' bounded entity analogous to the clear boundary proposed for the large mining extension? Given the scale of the proposed mining extension and the boundaries involved, Kol appears to be summoning up a discourse analogous to and substitutable for this large entity (see Strathern 1999, chapter 10). He did not indicate to Alphonse or I that this was his intention. He was concerned instead with the claims Ononge people might make with respect to what he knows to be Visi land. His personal interest, as expressed to me, was simple: 'I want to eat the money and die.' In other words, he views himself as an old man and wants to use the money from the compensation/rent to buy betelnut, pork, sugar and other excellent, sweet tasting things before he eventually dies. He claims those of Ononge who say it is their land are lying; he does not want them to 'eat' his money.[18]

But it was also clear that Kol knew that in a dispute about land, involving the mining company and government, one could not present a 'small' claim; one had to present a claim that would be seen and heard. This was as much about his local status as a great chief as it was about the size of the mining concern itself. For the boundaries of Visi to be seen and to be seen as persuasive, Kol had to summon up a narrative appropriate to the person(s) with whom such an interchange might occur. What he had made explicit was that the capacity of Tolukuma gold mine to determine boundaries did not rest with the mine alone. In his own unique way Kol was offering a challenge to how the present would appear and how the future might transpire.

Notes

1. I warmly thank all those in Visi who facilitated my initial research; to Alphonse Hega, Kol Usi and all of those of Yuvenise with whom I stayed during my most recent visit, I offer much gratitude.
2. The French Catholic missionaries established a station on land of Honong which they pronounce and write as Ononge. This is how all the places or homes (*em*) nearby the mission, and speaking the same dialect, have come to be referred (e.g. Evese, see map).
3. *Gab* is a multi-stage ritual which transforms persons (both singular and collective), through acts of reciprocal coercion among hosts and dancers, pig killers, and exchange partners (see Hirsch 1994: 700–2, for further elaboration).
4. Earlier last century Williamson noted the following attributes of *tidibe*. He lived in the extreme lower Auga Valley for three months – at Mafulu – with the French Catholic missionaries, several years after they established a station there in 1905. Williamson's rendering of *tidibe* as *Tsidibe* is because of the dialect variations.
    [T]here is a general belief among them in a mysterious individual named *Tsidibe [tidibe]*, who may be a man, or a spirit (they appear to be vague as to this), who has immense power, and *who once passed through their country* in a direction from east to west... They believe that it was *Tsidibe* who taught them all their customs, including dancing and manufacture, and that he ultimately reached and remained in the land of the white man, where he is now living; and that the superior knowledge of the white man in manufacture and especially in the making of clothes, has been acquired from him. The idea of his ultimate association with the white man can hardly, however, be a very ancient tradition. One of the Fathers was seriously asked by a native whether he had ever seen *Tsidibe*. They seem to think that he is essentially a beneficient being. They regret his having left their country, but they have no doubt as to this... As traces of his passage through their country they will show you extraordinarily shaped rocks and stones, such as fragments which

have fallen from above into the valley, and rocks and stones which have lodged in strange positions. (Williamson 1912: 265, emphasis added, quoted in Hirsch 1994: 703).

5. The names of various *tidibe* and ancestors have been used in different, brief, accounts I recorded. To avoid confusion I simply use 'he' as a generic to refer to all of these.

6. A *tobo*, a large gourd used to store seeds or to carrying water.

7. At the time of fieldwork during July–August 1999, I was only aware of an exploration license that had been granted to Dome Resources NL (this was granted during 1996 with an expiry date of 12/12/00). However, as Filer (1993: 4, emphasis added) noted in the socio-economic impact assessment of Tolukuma he produced, prior to actual mining operations, '[m]easured reserves at Tolukuma Hill Zone C are currently thought to guarantee a minimum mine life of nearly six years, but the developer is confident of *making further discoveries in adjacent areas which will extend this period*. This study needs to consider the possibility that mining may last twice or even three times as long as the period currently projected from the measurement of these reserves.'

8. See Hirsch 1995 for a discussion of the change of the place name to Taurama.

9. This is reference to the joined rivers of Ili and Mo, or Ilimo, boundary or 'mark' between Visi and Woitape, the home to the north. Mo is spoken of on the Visi side and Ili on the Woitape side.

10. See note 5 above.

11. The question mark indicates that Kol did not know the origins of these men: Omale, Kambisi or Woitape? The questioning was explicit in the way he told this portion of the narrative.

12. *Bolos* is a type of pandanus which has marks on the shell.

13. I have altered the name of this *tidibe*.

14. This is where further work between Alphonse and myself needs to be focused.

15. Visi is the name of a type of grass which is common in this area.

16. Kol and Yavi both married the sister of the other.

17. Or a 'part' of the person, such as within dreaming, when a person's spirit comes to see and know matters not visible while awake.

18. Compare a similar sentiment expressed by one of Stuart Kirsch's Yonggom associates with regards to the compensation payments from the Ok Tedi mine: 'I am an old woman. I don't have the strength to garden or make sago anymore. I want them to distribute the money quickly, so that I can taste some sugar before I die.' (Stuart Kirsch, personal communication).

3

Disputing Damage
Versus
Disputing Ownership in Suau

Melissa Demian

At a 1999 village court sitting in Isuisu, Western Suau,[1] Milne Bay Province, a land boundary dispute was brought before the magistrates. They refused to hear it, gently chastised the litigants for bringing them the 'wrong kind' of case, and instructed them to take their case to the land mediators instead. As a complement to this incident, at a land mediation one month later, one of the mediators said in his preamble to the proceedings: 'If you chop down a person's oil palm or kill them because of it, you have a court. If you're only fighting over whose oil palm it is, then you talk to me.' There was, in the formulations of both these officials, a clear distinction between the remits of the village court and the land mediators. This distinction has ramifications which extend not only to the cases before them, but to the flow of authority behind them, and it provides a background for the cases which I will present here. The magistrates and land mediator cited above had very clear ideas about the appropriate venue for debating ownership of land as opposed to an act resulting in harm to another person. While such notions will at least in part have been informed by the government-prescribed structures for dealing with both types of litigation, it may also be true that these structures have been so readily adopted because of their acceptability to Suau conceptions of relationships in a state of crisis or negativity, and the ideal shape of their resolution. However, it is important first to outline briefly the presence of 'the law' on the Suau Coast and the role of village court magistrates as its putative agents.

Law, ownership and dispute settlement

Statutory law as practised in Papua New Guinean local and district courts is as far from rural life as acts of Parliament, although police, as enforcers of the law, are disparaged for their inability or unwillingness to apprehend local *raskol* (the Tok Pisin term for violent criminals) and feared for the seeming arbitrariness of their activities.[2] Law as encountered in the village court is by definition 'customary law', that is, local usage operating under the auspices of state sanction, and within certain guidelines and restrictions also established by the state.

I come to the notion of ownership by way of land claims where one might expect the English term 'owner' to be employed, as indeed it sometimes is on the Suau Coast, along with the local term *tanuwaga*. These claims are distinct from other cases in which what appears as injury to property is actually treated as injury to persons, whose outcomes necessarily include the payment of compensation, and which fall within the jurisdiction of the village court. To explore further the material aspect of compensation for injury, I will also examine a case which is explicitly one of unmediated injury, that is, one in which a thing is not substituted for a person or part of a person.[3] The appearance and disappearance of 'property', in the sense of things owned, from these cases is meant as an illustration of the ways in which Suau imagine different modes of negativity to be resolvable.

Village court magistrates themselves define their work as being the maintenance of 'law and order', the English phrase kept intact and imported into Suau, which in turn refers to their embodiment of government interests, which presumably hold 'law and order' to be of paramount importance. Some magistrates even place themselves in a direct line of 'descent' from the patrol officers who stopped visiting the Suau Coast in the early 1970s. They wear badges, they are given preliminary training (but usually none after that), and in theory they can summon police from one of the government stations to carry out imprisonment orders. But many magistrates complain that these hypothetical connections are not backed by real efficacy: their pay is extremely low (K26/month in 1999) and their training minimal; furthermore police speedboats are chronically short of fuel, so imprisonment orders and other disciplinary actions are rarely carried out. The primary force behind their relationship to the government, then, is rhetorical and symbolic. This is not to downplay its significance for magistrates and litigants, but rather to specify its provenance and the limits of its capacity for 'real-world' effectiveness. Magistrates are caught in a double bind. They do not always have recourse to the persuasive powers of senior men adept at pig exchange and other transactions, and neither do they have the efficacy of the government at their disposal. One long-serving former magistrate dismissed his successor with the following statement, in the process outlining what he thought was key to the success or failure of a magistrate:

> In my opinion, if their thinking is very straight, if they're a person of integrity, okay, then they can have the magistrate's job. But that K. there, he has yet to find his straightness. All these men, you see, they'll just turn bad... A person could diminish their name that way. It's the same for councillors and magistrates. The law is the law: you have to have great integrity.

He also told me that magistrates have no defences against the malefactors they deal with, particularly sorcerers. Their only real authority lies in their moral fortitude and their wits, characteristics summed up in the word I have glossed as 'integrity' (*sibasiba*), a trait connoting intelligence, foresight and diligence. And the final part of his statement, *laugagayo hesana laugagayo*, literally translates as 'the name of law is law', 'law' being the gloss invariably offered by English speaking Suau for *laugagayo*. But in popular usage it appears to refer specifically to *prohibitions* – which may in fact be the aspect of government statutes which are most apparent to villagers. At a village meeting in Isuisu, the peace officer explained that 'Law [*laugagayo*] has two parts: the church side and the government side.' At his suggestion that perhaps Isuisu should have some laws of its own, one old man stood up and complained that there were too many laws already – 'don't do this, don't do that!' As far as this man was concerned, the only apparent interest of the government was to place restrictions on people.

The intended purpose of the Village Courts Act 1973 was twofold: to provide legal access to rural people, and to attempt to integrate custom and law (Scaglion 1990: 19) by creating a forum for the application of custom by local magistrates invested with authority by the state. The problem was then, and arguably still is, the assumption of a fundamental opposition between 'custom' and 'law'. I did not observe any such distinction in the operation of Western Suau village courts; rather, the issue preoccupying most people seemed to be negotiation between custom and *money*, which will be dealt with in more detail below. But the very fact that the activities of village courts and their magistrates vary so widely from province to province (Jessep and Luluaki 1994: 196) is arguably as much an indicator of the flexibility of the institution as it is of the difficulty of providing training and support for magistrates. While some courts have been reported to imitate as closely as possible the trappings and officialdom of local and district courts (Westermark 1986, Scaglion 1990), this was far from the case in Suau. There, magistrates typically conducted hearings at their houses, convened them whenever there was a sizeable enough backlog of cases or a single grave case such as sorcery, and rarely consulted the magistrates' handbook. Furthermore, the prohibitive cost of speedboat petrol (around K2/litre in 1999) meant that it was not always possible to muster the three magistrates necessary to hold a full court hearing, and so 'settlement hearings' with one or two magistrates acting as mediators have become increasingly common.[4] The preoccupations of litigants in Suau indicate an abiding concern with such 'customary' issues as bridewealth, sorcery, and strained relations between affines, but that they choose to prosecute these cases via an 'imposed' legal institution in the first place is instructive. It would appear that the law has been made to do the work of maintaining relationships in a manner acceptable to Suau disputants. It is the job of magistrates to decide which kinds of disputes are litigable not only in terms of what their remit covers under statutory law, but also in terms of local sensibilities. I wish to emphasise that village court disputes are primarily an arena for claims of *harm* done to persons directly through acts such as assault, sorcery, or slander, or indirectly through acts such as adultery, theft, or damage to personal property. They are ideally kept separate from disputes over land, as the two examples with which I opened illustrate. This is not to say conflicts over land do not sometimes spill over into the village court, particularly when land mediators are not available.[5] The breakdown below, from court records kept for the Western Suau subdistrict over seven years, illustrates some of the most common preoccupations of disputants. The subdistrict, with a population of roughly 1,000, is served by six village court magistrates and one clerk.

Subjects of dispute in Western Suau, 1992-99

Adultery	9
Assault	2
Cash debts	1
Court-related misdemeanours[6]	3
Damage to or theft of property	4
Land (including timber royalties)	2
Pig debts	2
Pig debts payable in cash	2
Sorcery	9
Threatening language	1

The emphasis on harm as a suitable subject for litigation carries with it a concomitant ideal for resolution. In Suau, what is brought to the village court is a 'problem', *pilipili*, which is an amplification of *pili*, 'complicated'. The problem or complication is then 'straightened', *hadudulai*, by means of a court or less formal mediation hearing. While not wanting to assume too much from terminology alone, there are further indications here of divergent approaches to the objects of disputes. One kind of dispute is over damage to persons and to ephemeral personal property, such as houses or canoes; this kind characteristically anticipates a compensation payment in the course of its resolution. The other kind of dispute is to do with conflicting claims over land, whose status as 'property' is evident in its separate terms of dispute, which may or may not include compensation .[7] This type does not appear to be the remit of 'law' as embodied in the village court. Aside from the fact that land mediation is a separate institution from the village court, it is important to bear in mind that land mediations are not necessarily concluded with the payment of compensation, and certainly do not assume it as a matter of procedure in the way that village courts do.

What all disputes have in common is that they are a public exhibit of relationships in a negative state. The village court is often a last resort for such problems, upon interventions by family members and/or the magistrate in his[8] capacity as mediator and representative of the state, along with the local government councillor. In any given case the magistrate or land mediator must convert a negative relationship into a positive one. A relationship that is not 'straight', that is one diverted or inverted by a history of conflict and complication, must be induced to traverse the correct path. A *hadudulai* can be an informal affair, overseen by a councillor, a pastor or some other village court official, and is used frequently for minor disputes, particularly intralineage ones. 'Straightening' in the village court, however, is usually only achieved by the levying of compensation, typically composed of a payment in pigs and a payment in cash. When I asked the former magistrate how he had decided what to fine people for compensation, meaning the severity of the payments, he instead answered with a formula for the *composition* of the payments: 'Custom, half, and money, half.' Two sides of economic life had to be attended to, just as two sides of the law must be attended to. And when he said that a magistrate's thinking must be straight, he meant possibly that court hearings are not so much about punishing inappropriate action as they are about re-establishing positive relations between the feuding parties by inducing the relations to appear by means of public dispute. Or he may have meant that relations in a negative state are inverted by means of the person of the magistrate, who cannot effect such a transformation if his own moral and intellectual capacities are in doubt. But the way in which any straightness is achieved in a case involving personal harm will invariably involve a transaction between the litigants – and it may be a one-way *or a reciprocal* transaction – which is an important factor in distinguishing it from cases of dispute over ownership.

I would like now to turn to the specifics of three cases. The first two are village court cases from the inland village of Leileiyafa and the third is an informal *hadudulai* or 'straightening' over land from the coastal village of Isuisu. Although they range in gravity from an altercation between affines in the first, to far-reaching issues of inheritance and stewardship in the last, the relationships in these cases can all be said to have been diverted from their appropriate path, that is, the intentions of other people for a particular person. They provide a useful test of the proposition that what happens in a village court hearing is qualitatively different from what happens in a dispute over land, and that this quality is most immediately visible in the conclusion of the case, rather than its 'origin'. The idea here is, on a smaller scale, what Riles has identified as 'discovering relationships where lawyers see rules' (Riles 1994: 631). Litigants in Suau are only too aware of the 'rules' ostensibly governing them. What is actually within their power to affect are, of course, the relationships.

Case 1: Vandalism

While many village court cases and unofficial mediations are to do with pigs, and most of these in turn are delinquent bridewealth debts, this was the only one in my experience which had been complicated by violence. Two families, from the hamlets of Gelugelu and Malatau, were holding a bridewealth repayment feast (*golisae'eno*), inclusive of three pigs to be brought from Gelugelu, the bride's hamlet, to the groom's parents at Malatau. One of the pigs was unusually large, and the people at Malatau felt unable to care for it properly. So they sent the pig-bearers to a third hamlet, Labapa'ana, for the groom's mother and stepfather to look after it. This largest, more prestigious pig in a *golisae'eno* prestation is understood to be the 'payment' to the father of the bride or groom for his nurturing work, and would therefore not be slaughtered for the feast but kept by the groom's (in this instance) parents. The smaller pigs, however, would ordinarily be slaughtered and consumed by the receiving lineage and their guests. But while the three pigs were in transit to Labapa'ana, the men from Malatau followed the pig-bearers to tell them not to kill the two smaller pigs. But they were too late; the pigs had been killed already. An argument ensued which escalated into a fight, culminating in the destruction of a house. At the subsequent village court hearing, the young men from Gelugelu who had 'rioted' at Labapa'ana were instructed to give a pig and K100 to the man whose house they had destroyed.

The compensation ordered in this case was specifically designed to serve two separate purposes. The hundred kina were intended to help rebuild the ruined house, I was told, and the pig was meant as a demonstration of respect (*ha'atiti*) for its owner. This was particularly apt, since an acceptable (if extreme) method of driving away unwanted affines is to burn their house and kill their pigs – or to threaten such action, which often is all it takes. The young men from Gelugelu had effectively accomplished half of such a threat, although their doing so was obviously not premeditated. But in this situation a compensation payment which had the capacity to add to both of these indicators of settledness (house and pigs) could, ideally, re-establish the goodwill and respect which ought to exist between affines. I want to make clear that the sentiments of those paying the compensation may or may not be relevant in the face of their payment. The fact that the money and pig changed hands was what mattered, because this was the visible manifestation of straightening. The movement of wealth alone was sufficient to demonstrate the normalisation of relations between Gelugelu and Labapa'ana hamlets, because all could see that these things were passing between them on a path imposed or imagined by the magistrate. The nature of this particular dispute – violence and compensation – lent itself well to conversion by means of the village court into a positive relationship. Not all cases are so straightforward, however, as the next example, in which the provisions of the village court may have been somewhat inadequate, will demonstrate. But the case was brought to court nonetheless, which suggests that the parties concerned thought it might be salvageable by taking this course of action.

Case 2: Wife-beating

Domestic violence is not uncommon in Suau. People are quick to lash out at one another physically and just as quick to forget the quarrel afterwards. The fact that this particular incident was taken to court probably owed as much to its politicisation by some of the witnesses as to its being something of a denouement in the struggling relations between the husband and wife involved.

Peter and Dawasi were a young couple with an uneasy history together. Dawasi, an in-married wife from the coast, displayed a barely-suppressed disdain for her 'backwards' inlander husband and his family. She had had a miscarriage the previous year, during which Peter did not visit her in hospital at all, and this she frequently cited as proof that he was not actually interested in being her husband. His parents had also failed to pay hers any bridewealth yet, and she was convinced he had used magic to attract and keep her with him, a suspicion I heard voiced by more than one coastal wife in Leileiyafa. They had been staying in her village, Nawabu, but not long after their return to Leileiyafa rumours began to circulate that Peter was sleeping with other women. Finally Dawasi accused him outright of impregnating a local girl, and he beat her with a piece of firewood. Her loud crying brought an instant response from other people in the hamlet, mostly women, who rushed to Peter and Dawasi's house. They stood about heatedly discussing what had happened while Peter stood at one corner of the kitchen staring at the wall and Dawasi knelt weeping at the other. This extremely tense scene was perhaps the first indication that matters had come to a head and could not proceed further without intervention. The *ex post facto* 'witnessing' of the beating by neighbours turned Peter and Dawasi's troubled marriage into public knowledge, whereas before it had only existed as gossip.

The problem was further complicated over the next few days, as two other coastal women counselled Dawasi to leave Peter and return to Nawabu. When she tried to do so, she was retrieved en route by a senior woman of Peter's lineage who insisted she stay until the impending village court hearing. She did so, and at the hearing, a week later, reiterated her catalogue of grievances against Peter. The 'other woman' in the case said she had also been deceived by Peter in collusion with the daughter of the woman who had prevented Dawasi from leaving. But when the magistrates asked Dawasi whether she wanted to stay with Peter or leave him, she said she would stay. Peter was instructed to kill a chicken and give a feast for Dawasi, and the two women who had advised Dawasi to leave before her case was heard were fined K10 each.[9]

About two months after her case was heard, Dawasi discovered she also was pregnant, and decided to go home to Nawabu and be cared for by her parents. Of her pregnancy she told me, 'This is my gift. His gift is from Gelugelu,' referring to the hamlet of the other woman Peter had got pregnant. This woman, however, would have nothing to do with Peter, refusing his offers to help maintain the daughter who was born some time later. He rejoined Dawasi back at Nawabu, and then they both went to stay in Alotau so that her pregnancy could be monitored at the hospital there. When I returned to Leileiyafa nearly two years later they and their small son were living in a new house in Peter's hamlet, and relations between them seemed to have improved.

Another feature of the case was that it became politicised by secondary actors. Following the beating, factions developed behind two senior women with a deep, abiding and public antipathy toward one another: the coastal woman who had encouraged Dawasi to leave Leileiyafa, and Peter's kinswoman who had brought her back. By claiming to keep Dawasi in Leileiyafa in order for the hearing to be held, this woman could support her errant kinsman and show up her rival as having gone against court procedure at the same time. On the whole, it was undoubtedly the sort of case in which, to borrow Young's words, 'ostensibly private delicts might be treated by a community to a form of "show trial," thereby injecting them with political significance.' (Young 1974: 49). As I mentioned before, the use of violence against wives by husbands is not unusual, and so the fact that this case was brought to the village court communicated several things to the village at large. One was the acknowledgement of the antagonism between the two senior women, which was a constant source of friction in the hamlet where they both lived. A concomitant of this was the fact that the woman who had told Dawasi to leave was penalised and the one who had made her stay was not, as if in warning that any further conflicts between them over such a sensitive issue might result in a certain loss of face for one of them. The final message was that wife-beating would not be sanctioned, but it is to be noted that Peter was not so much punished as made a spectacle of. His penalty, to organise a feast for his wife, reflected the very public nature of his transgression, the fact that it had been 'felt' throughout the village. He was required to demonstrate his contrition toward Dawasi as flagrantly as he had demonstrated his anger toward her, thereby keeping the status of their relationship on the same broad frequency. It was no surprise to anyone, then, that neither of them stayed in Leileiyafa for very long after the quarrel and court hearing. Perhaps the court hearing was 'successful' in that it allowed Dawasi to choose whether or not to stay married to Peter in a publicly authorised environment, although her discomfort at being the object of so much attention was painfully evident throughout the hearing. I cannot help but speculate as to whether Dawasi chose to stay with Peter because of the effectiveness of the court and the penalty it handed down, or because of her embarrassment at being so openly fought over. She may have decided against divorce because the negativity generated by her and Peter's feud had affected so much of her social field.

This last case presents something of a challenge to my argument that the job of a magistrate is to convert negative relations into positive ones. But by 'positive', I do not necessarily mean an amicable, peaceable or otherwise 'friendly' sense of the term. I am trying to move away from a model of dispute settlement that assumes concord as a normative state whose disturbance must be rectified (see Greenhouse 1982: 68). It was abundantly obvious that Peter and Dawasi's relationship could not be made good overnight, and it was probably the birth of their son more than anything else which enabled them to be 'serious' about their marriage. But by the imposition of an act of compensation, what the magistrates did, in both of the above cases, was ensure that *relations still existed* between the parties involved, if only in the form of pigs and money, or a feast, moving from one to the other. A positive relationship, in this context, is one that is still 'alive', still active. The compensation transaction, while imposed by the village court, sees to it that the road between the transgressor and the transgressed-against does not disappear for lack of use.

Magistrates are only capable of emphasising and shoring up prior relationships; they cannot invent them or rule them out of existence. Far from forfeiting any 'rights' he might have had to contact with Dawasi, Peter was made to confront the very relationship he had corrupted by means of the feast he made for his wife. This calls to mind the former magistrate's attributing similar properties (because he assumed their commensurability) to custom and money. Instead of rights being manipulated in court, we see objects – indigenous and exogenous forms of wealth – which share an analogous consumptibility. The fact that pigs and money are so frequently paired as compensation payments in Suau is no accident: the one can be eaten, the other can be spent, and according to some people money can be added 'on top of' a small pig to make it larger for the purposes of exchange. Neither pigs nor money are imperishable in the way shell wealth and stone axe blades were, but these items were emblematic of a different epoch. The order of the day now is objects which are 'used up' at a certain point in their lifetime as valuables, and are divisible and distributable, further attributes they do not share with 'old-time' valuables. The fact that pigs are complementary to cash in village court transactions is a creative reading of the court's jurisdiction. As an 'imposed' institution, it must perforce conduct its business with the new form of wealth, money – but as it is meant to deal also with custom, it appends wealth in the form of pigs. The result is a transaction of rather a different order from 'customary law', as strictly speaking it is neither custom nor law. That is, it is not custom because it is generated by a new institution, and it is not law because it is to do with the realignment of relationships rather than the enforcement of 'rules' or 'norms'. But are there cases in which compensation is not the best way to achieve this realignment or straightness? My final example was such a case, and demonstrates that compensation was explicitly avoided for a reason, which in turn may point to some possible insights about the nature of claiming ownership in Suau.

Case 3: Whose trees?

Thomas was building a new house. Because it was the holiday period, which is typically when relatives working in the towns come back to the village, Thomas's brother Ruatoka was home from Lae. Ruatoka owned a walkabout sawmill and a dinghy, but had left both of them with his affines in another village to the west of Isuisu. So he brought the sawmill in the dinghy to Isuisu, and he and Thomas cut down two large trees: one for Thomas's house, and one for the house of an older couple, Felicia and Pola. There was an objection to the felling of this second tree, which resulted in a *hadudulai* to sort out the problem. The short-term agreement reached at the 'straightening' was that Thomas and Ruatoka would cut no more trees without consulting the other people who claimed authority[10] over the land on which the trees grew. But the more fundamental question of who was actually *tanuwaga* of the land, its manager or 'boss' as Suau often gloss it, was not resolved, and has every likelihood of erupting again. What follows are the salient points of the case, according to various disputants with whom I discussed it separately.

Sibawa and Louisa are parallel cousins, and are therefore classified as siblings in Suau. They claimed to be *tanuwaga* of the land abutting the Dea River where the timber was cut, either through their fathers who were local men or through Louisa's mother.[11] They both told me their objection was solely to the cutting of the second tree; Sibawa said that Thomas had only asked permission to cut a tree for himself. But they were satisfied with the assurance that no more would be cut, and said they would not ask for payment for the second tree.

Thomas located the problem with Louisa's husband Reuben; although Reuben's lineage comes from a village quite some distance from Isuisu, it is not uncommon for men in Suau to make land claims 'on behalf of' their wives. Thomas and Reuben are cross-cousins, and Thomas claimed that because Reuben's father was already dead, Thomas could assert authority over him because he stands in a (rarely invoked) classificatory father–son relationship to him since Thomas's mother has birth order precedence over her brother, Reuben's father. He said also that he had lectured the complainants (Sibawa, Louisa and Reuben) that what they were worried about was *land*, while he was talking about *logs*, as if to imply that this posed no threat to their claim.

Ruatoka told me that 'somebody' had actually demanded payment for the trees, and while he would not name this person, it seemed likely to have been Reuben, because he was the only disputant involved whom Ruatoka did not specifically mention by name. Ruatoka said that he had been willing to pay, but warned Thomas that it would set a precedent, so the next time this person asked them for help, they would have to ask *him* for payment. 'It would put the whole relationship into question,' he said. I hazarded that it would make kin look like non-kin. He smiled and said, 'That's it exactly.' While such an action may be more accurately described as turning consanguines into affines, Ruatoka's point was that paying for the trees would have been an undesirable exhibit of differentiation between members of a family who should have been 'of one mind' (*nua esega*) about the appropriate stewardship of the Dea River land and disposal of its products.

There were several other subtexts to this dispute. One was the fairly constant anxiety in Thomas and Ruatoka's family over 'jealousy' because of their high level of education and employment, and the consequent access to coveted equipment like dinghies, sawmills, and the fuel to run them. Isuisu is, on the whole, a far more cosmopolitan village than Leileiyafa: almost everyone under the age of twenty has at least some schooling, several people have made marriages to other provinces, and when those working in towns or boarding at school came home for the holidays, the population of the village increased by nearly half. But even by these standards Thomas and Ruatoka are wealthy: six of the ten siblings in their immediate family have salaried jobs, including Ruatoka who is a university lecturer. So arguments over access to trees may also have been 'about' arguments over access to other resources in the family, namely the ones put to use rather ostentatiously in order to fell and saw the timber for Thomas's house. In addition, authority over trees has very recently become linked to the ability to make money from trees, as the latest timber extraction scheme is mooted in villages all along the coast. And lastly, the question of why the second tree for Felicia and Pola was cut became another subject of conflicting accounts. Thomas and Ruatoka's youngest sister told me there had been a problem with the sawmill in the first few days – it wouldn't cut straight – and it was concluded that this was because their father, who died in 1997, was unhappy about the proceedings. Felicia, who had stood in a 'funeral executor' (*wolisau*) relationship to Thomas and Ruatoka's father, went to his grave to placate him by saying it was only a few trees being cut to house his children, nothing more. After this the sawmill functioned properly, so the tree was cut to thank Felicia for her services. But when I mentioned this version of events to Ruatoka he looked perplexed and said no, it was just because Felicia and Pola were distant relatives and it was decided to help them because they were also building a new house.

Where then is the truth in all this? Why was the second tree cut, who lodged the complaint at its being cut, and whose claim to authority over the trees was the strongest? That people were describing the same set of events was secondary to the fact that they were claiming different sources of causality, and different ways of privileging their claims over those of others. 'The truth' was not a matter of proof of ownership, but of teasing out a configuration of managerial relations from a tight mesh of consanguines and affines that most suited everyone for the time being – until the next conflict over trees arose. In the end, no payment was made to anybody in this case; it was not one which could be resolved by allocating compensation as in the previous cases. As Ruatoka had pointed out, the making of a payment would have had long-term ramifications which were probably not in anybody's interests. Everyone involved in the dispute was related to everyone else in some capacity, confirming the complaint I frequently heard in Isuisu that too many people had married 'too close to home' for the past two or three generations, thereby muddying the waters of inheritance. At issue was not so much ownership of land as authority over it, and over the interests of other members of the landholding lineage. Furthermore, there was Thomas's differentiation between 'land' and 'logs' to contend with. Not trees, it should be noted, but logs – there is no terminological difference in Suau, but Thomas used English to make this particular point. So was he suggesting that the products of land are secondary to land itself, are possibly more 'property-like' because more ephemeral? Was Ruatoka also suggesting that introducing payment into the equation would render the trees more like property, bring up the element of damage to property, and thereby shift the register of relations between the parties involved? I cannot presume to know what the brothers intended by their pronouncements, but more important to me was the fact that it was Thomas's framing of the problem as one of authority-over-trees rather than ownership-of-land, and Ruatoka's remark about the risks inherent in making a payment for the trees, which provided a means of understanding why land disputes are substantively different from disputes over harm to persons, and why it makes good sense for Suau to uphold the distinction between them handed down by government. What would test this distinction would of course be an environmental degradation case, in which damage to land and damage to persons might be made commensurate. So far, the Suau Coast has been fortunate enough not to require such a test of its litigant sensibilities.[12]

Conclusion

In one of the earlier studies of the introduction of Western-style legal proceedings to Papua New Guinea, Peter Lawrence identified the different aims of Papua New Guinean dispute settlement but may have misread the kind of sociality underpinning these aims: 'In the New Guinea system, there is no concept of *fiat justitia, ruat coelum* but a clear recognition that the sky must be kept up. In settling a dispute, the aim is to restore the social order, or to patch up relationships that have been broken or damaged.' (Lawrence 1969: 34). The idea that there is a kind of social solidarity which can be 'broken' by disputes persists still, dogging debate on the effectiveness of village courts in Papua New Guinea. I hope to have gone some way toward demonstrating that the preoccupation of magistrates with turning negative relations into positive ones, precludes any such notion of relations being somehow broken or disrupted, for the reason that relations *cannot* be broken, but they can go awry and manifest a destructive rather than a productive potential. In such cases, magistrates may use compensation as a means of making straight a strayed relationship. But compensation itself draws our attention towards cases in which it is *not* implemented, and compels us to ask why it is not considered appropriate in those cases. While it might be tempting to assume that land disputes are the most likely to include compensation as part of their outcome, this turns out not to be the case. It may be that to require compensation would also require 'owners', persons who stand in a fixed possessive relationship to the land in question, and who could be harmed as a consequence of harm done to the land. But *tanuwaga*, persons with authority, by definition do not 'possess' but rather orchestrate, cause others to act under their influence, and furthermore their occupation of this role is always negotiable. 'Owners' have a prior existence to what is owned, otherwise we would have great difficulty with the concepts of rights and dispossession. But a *tanuwaga* can only exist in the presence of land to be managed, and other members of a lineage over whom to exert authority. For their part, village court magistrates, who specialise in knowing how to fit the compensation to the crime, make it a point to steer clear of land disputes as far as possible, because issues of authority cannot be resolved in the same way as issues of damage. Both have their origins in relations which have gone from straight-ness to an unfavourable state of complexity: what differentiates them are their conclusions.

The 'modes of negativity' which I mentioned earlier in this chapter are exemplified but not limited by the cases I have presented here. Each case deals with potentially destructive relations in a particular configuration of persons and property: injury done to a person through the medium of property, injury done directly to a person, and conflict over property in the absence of injury. In the first case ownership is treated as an inalienable relation between a person and his house, such that the twofold nature of compensation addresses both the damage to his house and the damage to respect for his person. In the second case injury is inflicted in an unmediated fashion on the person of a wife, so that compensation is accordingly meant to restore relations of concord between her and her husband. And in the final case property appears again, but in a different form – compensation must be avoided in order to maintain an 'injury-free' tone to negotiations among disputing members of the same lineage. Were injury to be acknowledged, the lineage will have failed to demonstrate its being 'of one mind' about the disposal of its property. In this final case the nature of ownership is something more than inalienable. What is 'owned' here is nothing less than land, which because it occupies a unique category of property, cannot even be fought over in the same way as other kinds. The status of *tanuwaga* is so contingent upon birth order, who is alive or dead, who is resident on the land or not, when and how the land came into the lineage, whether and why the land is claimed through the father's side, that disputing over this form of property becomes a question of identity as much as it is a question of ownership. Land disputes, whether formal or informal, are not so much about establishing who the land belongs to, as it is about establishing who the land *is* at that particular juncture in time. Such a form of ownership is by its very nature extremely difficult to resolve. In the final case, there was no conclusion. It is, for its disputants, an issue of ongoing debate.

Notes

1. By Western Suau I refer not only to the administrative district known by this name, but also to the linguistic and cultural subdivision called Duiduileu by Suau-speakers, that is, the stretch of coastline (plus its hinterland) from Saga'aho westward to Gadaisu near the border with Central Province.

    Fieldwork was conducted in Leileiyafa between August 1996 and October 1997, and in Isuisu between August 1999 and January 2000. I am grateful to all the people of these two villages for their help and hospitality, but special thanks go to my hosts, the family of Saunia Beliliso in Leileiyafa and the family of Mamari Eseroma in Isuisu.

2. For example, I was told that in 1995 police had rounded up all young men with a certain type of haircut, and jailed them on suspicion of belonging to a raskol gang. By the time of my first arrival in 1996, this story had blossomed into a rumour that the next time police came through the area, they would shoot anyone with this haircut.

3. Apologies are due here to Marilyn Strathern, whose concept of mediated and unmediated exchange (1988:177–8) I have corrupted. The principle is the same, of course; I have simply invoked its negative potential (see Munn 1990).

4. These factors would appear to challenge Paliwala's (1982) hypothesis that the more contact a Papua New Guinean community has with Western institutions and preoccupations, the more formal and 'Westernised' its village court will be. Suau has had an ongoing relationship with Europe and Australia since the nineteenth century, beginning in earnest with the arrival of the London Missionary Society and bêche-de-mer merchants in the 1870s, followed by rubber and coconut plantations planted to support the Australian administration's head tax. In the twentieth century the Second World War also had a significant impact on the Suau Coast, when men were recruited in their hundreds to work as domestic labourers for American and Australian soldiers stationed on Milne Bay. In spite of the influences of mission, government and military activity, I observed none of the self-conscious bureaucracy and mimicry of Australian-style courts reported by Paliwala for Simbu Province, which remained uncontacted by Europeans until the 1930s.

5. It has further been my experience that a land mediation is a much more elaborate production than a village court dispute in Suau. Among the considerations of disputants when choosing to whom to take their problem must therefore be the expense, planning and travel (for far-flung kin) involved in a full-blown land mediation.

6. These may include disobeying a summons or interfering with court officials in some way.

7. On the occasions when compensation for land is discussed, the term almost invariably used is 'royalties', which suggests that the notion of compensating someone for land use may have been introduced or popularised by oil palm and timber companies.

8. All village court magistrates on the Suau Coast at the time of my research were men. There is of course no law prohibiting women from being appointed to the post, and the magistrates I spoke to conceded that such a thing was certainly conceivable, but public office does not tend to be the way in which Suau women engage with the political life of a village.

9. Fines are payable to the court officials themselves, as distinct from compensation which is paid to the complainant, ostensibly to cover the running costs of the court hearing – although one of the women fined in this case remarked sourly to me afterward that the fine was probably levied in order to keep the magistrates in tobacco. Their fines were not inconsequential. The only income available to both of them would have come from selling mangrove crabs at the market in Alotau or at the oil palm plantation at Sagarai, and K10 would comprise at least half of a typical market day's takings. As it would also cost K10–20 for a return journey to the market, these fines could easily represent an entire crabbing-and-market expedition, or two very long days of work.

10. In using the term 'authority' I have in mind the Suau concept of *gigiboli*, which can mean variously heat, charisma, and power; when used with an 'alienable' possessive marker it denotes authority over another person or a set of circumstances.

11. Inheritance through one's father is not quite a legitimate claim in Suau without mitigating factors to override the matrilineal default, but there are a number of such factors to which people can appeal, such as having made large contributions to important events within the father's matrilineage or adoption of a child from that lineage.

12. This may only be due to the absence of 'development' projects with more than localised environmental effects, however. Clear-cutting of timber around the villages of Gadaisu and Modewa, and pesticides and weed-killers used on oil palm grown in the Sagarai Valley, have caused a certain amount of misery in their respective localities, but none of it is far-reaching or conclusive enough to inspire a 'mine-sized' compensation claim, for example.

4

Land, Trees and History
Disputes Involving Boundaries and Identities in the Context of Development

James Leach

This chapter sets out two disputes over a single piece of land.[1] These disputes, between two separate Nekgini villages on the Rai Coast in Madang Province, occurred because of the heightened interest in the piece of land due to a perceived connection with 'development'.[2] The land was seen as facilitating one set of people's access to the world of development and money, instead of another's. This incited the descendants of previous owners, who otherwise had been unconcerned to regain the land, to make claims over it and its products.

It appears that land is a disputed resource here. However, I will argue that it is land involved in particular relationships which is perceived as a resource, and thus the land itself *refers to* the site of real valuation – generative or productive relations between persons. This links the case with the approach of the chapters in this volume. That is, the authors of the chapters contained here take the claims people make, rather than the objects claimed, as the starting point for analysis. This means attention is given to the transactions in which such claims are embedded. Presuming transactions as a starting point allows freedom to describe in detail how specific transactions, and peoples' concerns within them, generate value.

In this case it was the particular relationships in which the land came to have new effect, promise a new outcome, or facilitate relationships with significant others, that was the origin of the dispute on both occasions. Land itself, one might say, is not the significant resource. It is land shown to be productive that is of interest. This of course comes about through use. Use involves others, either in assisting with the productive endeavour, or in recognising the value of what has been produced.

These issues (use, production, recognition, legitimacy) relate directly to ownership. If land is claimed through recognition of its productivity, and this in turn depends on marshalling productive relations with other persons beyond the immediate owners, then notions of boundaries between land owning groups begin to look problematic (see Hirsch, this volume). Making relations beyond one's own group is valued, as it is in these relationships that work, productivity, and power are recognised. Land is not a resource in and of itself. Nor in this area do corporate groups which endure over time cohere around land ownership (see Lawrence 1984; Leach 2000). Idioms of connection (kinship) are not based on the transmission of bio-genetic substance among Nekgini speakers. Thus descent as transmission of identifiable essence through procreation is not the principle around which people associate. I submit that there are not 'clans' (that is, corporate groups which endure for more than three generations due to the transmission of substance at birth from one parent), nor other corporate groups which have *a priori* or *sui generis* control over land among Nekgini speakers. Land is not owned out of context, out of history, and out of the particular relations that make it valuable. There is an old anthropological insight here; ownership is a function of relations between persons with reference to things, and not between people and things (Hann 1998).

However there is also a specific point which can be made more strongly in this case. That is, these relations between persons are not fixed by biology (that is, connected indissolubly to the identity of the biogenetic substance passed from generation to generation), nor are they in some way attached, as part of identity, to descent groups (although this link may be made elsewhere in PNG).

Euro-American folk understandings assume that substance is inherited from both parents. English common law follows this, and embellishes it by giving one line of transmission (paternal) precedence over the other for the purposes of succession. The substance passed from parents to children during conception is thought of as an essence. Because there is an inheritance here, it is possible to think of this essence as an immutable and constant element. It is the perceived continuity of this essence which puts the link of identity between parent and child beyond question. A further link is made between this essence, the identity of the child, and rights over the property (or position in the case of male children and their father) of the parents. A link is made between essence as biogenetic inheritance, identification though this essence with ones' predecessors (and their siblings and children), and rights over property. This set of connections should not be automatically imported, as an emphasis on descent, wherever clans may be identified in PNG. It certainly makes no sense to do so among Nekgini speakers, where although people are capable of listing four or five generations of (usually male)[3] ancestors, clans (corporate politico-jural groups based on descent) defined by the criteria of minimal coherence through time, do not exist.

It is this model of transmission of essence, linked to identity, and therefore property, which is at the heart of the modelling of social organisation currently favoured by resource developers assisting with the incorporation of land groups on the Rai Coast. 'Clans' are being defined through reference to descent, the assumption being that because people give genealogical information which more readily identifies their male ancestors than their female ancestors, people connected through paternal descent share an essence which gives them their identity (patrilineages) and control over property (land).[4]

In the Euro-American modelling, this 'essence' is hidden in people's bodies. Hence the need for the law to embellish folk understandings with rules about how succession and transmission of property are to occur. The law makes explicit the connections assumed to be innate (implicit in people's bodily make-up). It recognises and makes visible the shared essence of identity between parents and children. The connection is presumed to be *prior to*, and *independent of*, any actions people may take. This set of ideas enables the link between descent, corporate groups and land ownership to seem plausible. In this view, merely gathering information on descent ought then to give information about land owning groups. I show here that this is not an appropriate approach to Rai Coast social organisation. In fact, it may not be relevant to the context in which corporate or descent groups appear in Papua New Guinea more generally (see Wagner 1974; Strathern 1988).

My position is that Nekgini speakers do not rely for their identity on the transmission of an essence at birth. Group identity is based on the constitution of the group in active exchange relations with others. Ownership or control of land is dependent upon this method of definition, and thus unavoidably involves relations with, and obligations to, others. Corporation through descent is just not the appropriate description for the groups formed by this process. Boundaries are made in ways that do not require, as their underlying rationale, there to be an immutable essence to identity, or link this to exclusive control over land or property. Although land and places are *central* to Nekgini speakers' identities, the connection between descent, ownership of land and identity, are not outside history (as one might say is true of the connection between biogenetic inheritance, corporate identity and control over particular lands are in the model of rights based on descent identity). They are constantly renegotiated, regenerated and brought to new effect, in the context of a shifting social field.

It is to demonstrate the mechanisms of this control over land, without positing the ownership of land as part and parcel of the kind of descent which produces corporate and enduring groups, that is one of the aims of this chapter. The other aim is to demonstrate ethnographically that all production in the region necessarily generates connections which are not severed, or even dealt with, in the immediate transaction which results from production (gardening, manufacture of objects, rearing of children). Obligations are generated in productive and reproductive activity which go beyond the transaction which is the focus of production. How to deal with legitimate claims which are created by production, yet go beyond the immediate transacting parties, is a more general problem for Papua New Guinean ownership regimes as the nation enters the new century (Banks and Ballard 1997; Filer 1997).

I conclude by linking my two themes. That is, I show how the dynamics of claims and ownership among Nekgini speakers are part of the ongoing regeneration of placement and identity. Wider lessons might be drawn about the imposition of models of corporate groups as enduring land owning entities in the context of resource rent distribution, from this and other material (Weiner 1998).

In what follows, I set out ethnographically the two disputes mentioned at the outset. By ethnographically I mean that I provide context in the specific sense of following up and drawing out the connections that the actors themselves see motivating their statements and claims. The names of certain people and groups have been changed.

Background: Social Organisation and Land

Nekgini social organisation is based around the Nekgini term *palem*.[5] A *palem* is a residential group who have demonstrated their connection in working together to produce an affinal payment. Affinal payments must always be made from one's place of residence. People of this place of residence become known as the people of 'the name of the piece of land', e.g. Reite *palem*. Children who reside together in a *palem* are classified as siblings, whatever their respective parents' relationship.

Land is passed on from fathers to their sons.[6] As *palem* generate siblingship, it is usual for groups of brothers and their unmarried sisters, who share adjacent land, to reside together. Yet it is not the *palem* that own land. Rather people in a hamlet bring the land they inherited from their fathers into the service of other hamlet members for joint ventures. The quintessential example of a joint hamlet venture is the staging of an affinal payment. It is the successful completion of this payment that turns the hamlet group into a *palem* group. Marriage is virilocal (wives move to the hamlet of their husband and garden on his land). Male landholding and virilocal marriage result in hamlet sites, and therefore *palem* sites, that do not necessarily change rapidly. It is both acceptable and in many ways preferable to use the *passae* (male cult house) and hamlet site of one's father. Without rigidity in their recruitment, *palem* often have histories of many generations. But the history is one of a *site* that gives its name to those making a *palem* there. Newcomers and their children are accommodated as *palem konaki* (one *palem*). Their children are siblings to those of other residents. This gives a form of coherence, an appearance of a lineage, without reference to biogenetic inheritance of substance. It also means that corporation is *regenerated* through reproductive processes which link the work of agriculture and production to the nurture of children. Descent does not figure strongly in the coherence of *palem* groups, as production and reproduction are aspects of the same process. The connections of kinship are not fixed by the inheritance of substance, but by joint work between male and female hamlet members in the production of children (see also Ingold 2000).

There are levels of inclusiveness to *palem* names, usually in proportion to their depth of history. Thus the name Reite, which now is an (official) administrative generalisation, and one which people from seven existent hamlets use to describe themselves as a 'village', was a historically distant *palem* name. All natal residents of the seven hamlets claim some connection to this overarching place of origin. New *palem* arise in each generation, as hamlet fission, often in the context of marriage, occurs. For example, in the words of a senior man, 'we are all [originally] from Ripia *palem*, but us lot went and lived on clay, so we are called Ripia Nalasis, or just Nalasis [*nala* – ground, *sis* – soft]'. Within Reite, there are many *palem* names.

Serieng is an overarching name for the next administrative village to the east. It also contains many *palem* names, some of which are memories from the past which still connect people as inheritors of land which belonged to siblings, some of which are still in use. Teva, for example, which features in the disputes that follow, is a historically distant *palem* site, and thus like Ripia, many people claim connection as siblings through it or as children of people who came from there. Tapuwang, like Nalasis, is a more recent *palem* site which only some people within Teva claim to have come from.

Pieces of land named <u>Posondaring</u> and <u>Isik Guhung</u> were ceded to ancestors of people in Reite-Ripia-Nalasis *palem* by people from Serieng-Teva-Tapuwang, for 'unknown reasons', at least three generations before the present. Teva and Nalasis have intermarried since before this time, and they share a number of common intangible resources. That is, spirit voices and designs for certain ritual objects have passed between them in the past, and continue to be shared today. They ideally co-operate and respect one another as cross-cousins (or the descendants of affines). It was the sharing of these resources that was called into question by the disputes over <u>Posondaring</u> and <u>Isik Guhung</u>.

The Disputes

1

When the plans for a road from the coast were being debated with the machine operators in 1988, the favoured route through Reite lands took the road over land which had been ceded to Nalasis (Reite) in previous generations for unspecified 'services rendered'.[7] Reite people gave permission for the developers to follow their chosen route over <u>Posondaring</u> and <u>Isik Guhung</u>. However, the route also took the road, for a few metres, onto another piece of land called <u>Maiyaparung</u>. When the village leader of Reite (*komiti*) approached Teva men about this encroachment, they said that the issue was much more substantial than he was allowing. They claimed <u>Posondaring</u> and <u>Isik Guhung</u> were theirs also.

Meetings followed, and I set out here the issues that were considered relevant and admissible as evidence in this case. The senior Nalasis man (Nalsen) recounted how in the time of the colonial government/*luluai*,[8] Reite people used to keep the road between Serieng and Reite clear of weeds and bush all the way to a place called <u>Imburang</u>. Serieng would meet them there, working up from their village. Nalasis people, who had close ties with their maternal kin in Serieng *palem*, also made gardens on <u>Maiyaparung</u>, and Nalsen had actually resided on Serieng lands close to <u>Imburang</u> so his maternal kin could offer him protection from threats to his life from other *palem* in Reite. These precedents had been kept to during the time of local government councils, when local committee members (*komiti*) organised community work. Thus when the road was planned, and was to stay on the Reite side of <u>Imburang</u>, the *komiti* of Reite gave it the go-ahead. But Serieng people did not want the road to pass through their lands. It was said by Reite people that they did not want a road to go that way *at all*, because many Serieng *palem* had relocated to be close to another road from the coast which ran parallel, and about 8 km to the east, of the proposed Reite road. Serieng youth protested against the planned route, and said the road could not be built. Moreover, they would take back their lands beyond <u>Imburang,</u> including <u>Maiyaparung</u> and <u>Posondaring/Isik Guhung,</u> if Reite pushed this matter.

Nalsen told his kin that they could not make a fuss about the return of <u>Maiyaparung</u> beyond <u>Imburang</u>. Their work on the footpaths and gardens of the area gave them some claim, but perhaps this was not strong enough to pursue. However, Posondaring and Isik Guhung had been given to Wamu, the great-grandfather of a living Nalasis man, Edward. These areas were not to be returned. At the time these places had been ceded to Wamu, Tapuwang also gave Wamu and his descendants use of certain forms of *kastom* (knowledge, procedures and powerful ways of doing things including designs). These items of *kastom* were a spirit voice (tune) called Masapting (*kaapu neng masapting*), a design for a long decorated bamboo pole (*tse'sopung*) which protrudes from the roof of the men's house during ceremonial activity (*tse'sopung kau sareining*), a form of planting (*hokung*) which is placed in the centre of a taro garden (*wasimung hokung*) and a tune to be used when dragging new slit-gong drums from their place of manufacture to their place of revelation (*sambing*). Nalsen said that if the Serieng youth took back Posondaring and Isik Guhung, Edward would also rightly give up these items of *kastom*. But this was categorically not to happen for the following reason.

Nalsen had been given protection by Serieng as a young man. People from the other *palem*s of Reite were threatening him, and he moved to the western edge of Serieng lands for a time. In addition, he had found his wife among the girls of Serieng. At this time, he had gained knowledge of this area and its history. These youth were not to try and overrule his authority. With conformation from a Serieng ancient called Panun, the history of the ceding of the land was established. In the time of their great grandparents (*sambai*), a woman (Yanaring) from Tapuwang *palem*, an offshoot of the larger and older Teva *palem*, was married to the Nalasis man named Wamu. It was the father of this women, a man called Sombee, that had given the land at Posondaring and Isik Guhung to Wamu and his wife, along with the items of *kastom*. There were no living members of Tapuwang *palem* other than one old woman married into another Teva *palem*. She confirmed this history.

As the people known as Tapuwang had no direct descendants from the site of their *palem*, their lands passed to their brothers in other Teva offshoot *palem*s. They claimed that Tapuwang was not another set of people, they were all Teva together, and thus they had a claim over their deceased kin's land. When there appeared to be a benefit from this land, these Teva *palem* members realised they did not know what arrangements had been made (items given in payment) for the land, and yet Reite were about to gain great advantage from it. Roads are often seen as highly significant conduits of power and advantage in rural PNG (for an example and explanation of this widespread perception, see Hirsch 1994).[9] Teva men said that they did not know what their ancestors had received, and Nalasis could not tell them this information, so Nalasis were told not to go onto this land anymore, or use it in any way.

In the meetings, Nalsen responded by saying, 'It is true that you do not know what our ancestors gave to your ancestors. You do not know what their "promise" (*promis*) was based on, and for that reason, you cannot claim the land back. The committee for land demarcation has told us that if your ancestors promise something, you cannot reverse this on a whim. These two pieces of land belong to Edward. Because you have no knowledge of the arrangements between the parties we can assume there was *kastom* involved, and you may not question the authority of such a transaction.'

At this, Serieng withdrew, and said that the road could be built over <u>Posondaring</u> and <u>Isik Guhung</u>, but that Reite people must not venture any further onto Serieng lands.

2

While working in Reite village during 1995, I was able, through the interest of the Papua New Guinea National Museum and Art Gallery in Port Moresby and the British Museum,[10] to make a collection of everyday items of contemporary material culture. This allowed an opportunity to see and record data about how objects were made, and it also enabled me to put some money directly into the hands of village people. Although the amounts were modest, I had to be very careful to make sure each household had some task and therefore was included in the project. Yet I had to put limits on who could be included (the money and time available were limited), and such arbitrary decisions (I decided to offer inclusion in the project to all households in Reite) do not always meet with the understandings of connection and obligation others may call upon. I make this comment specifically in the context of Rai Coast ethnography.

One of the items to be constructed was a slit-gong drum, made from the hollowed trunk of a particular softwood rainforest tree. As it happened, it was Edward who offered to lead the construction; a large undertaking, as a tree needed to be felled. The rest of the tree had to be marked up and made into slit-gongs also. Nekgini speakers do not waste such wood, and ancestral or spiritual sanction could be expected from not making use of the whole trunk once it had been felled following the particular set of procedures (*kastom*) required to turn the logs into entities with a 'voice'. All in all, most men in the village became involved, and the heavily 'ritualised' process of construction took nearly three months.[11] The tree was felled, and construction took place on the land known as <u>Isik Guhung</u>. When, in retrospect, I questioned Edward and the village *komiti* about the wisdom of using this land, they replied that that they thought the argument about it had been resolved years before in the context of the road.

Once the process was complete, and the drums were dragged to their moment of revelation in the hamlets of Reite, people began to prepare for the feast required for the spiritual powers which had assisted in the process. At this point, a letter arrived from Serieng, followed a couple of hours later by a group of people from there. With them came the local magistrate, a Serieng man himself. The letter began, 'We are not concerned with [will not take any notice of] promises made by people who have died. We are not prepared to hear what you have to say. We have heard that you have made slit-gong drums on our land. We hear you have made eight slit-gongs. We demand that you pay for these slit-gongs immediately.'[12]

Edward responded by calling the names of Teva people who had shown him the boundaries of the land which he had inherited. The name of Panun, and of Nalsen (both now deceased) were included as authority from each *palem*. Edward explained that Panun had shown him the actual tree he had cut, saying he had weeded it so it would grow well for Edward.

The complainant from Teva said that he knew it was Teva land. No one had been able to list the wealth that had been given by Nalasis for the use of it. Teva also knew that I (Leach) would take all these slit-gongs and sell them for a large amount of money. He wanted me, and Nalasis, to pay for what we had taken from his land from the profit on the slit-gongs. Several hours of sometimes angry discussion followed. The evidence was sifted through, and the conclusion of the previous dispute was revisited. At one point the magistrate suggested that they leave the dispute over land for land mediation, and concentrate on what had been made on the land. Nalasis responded saying that this was absurd, as the basis of their use of the tree had been their knowledge that they owned the land. In anger, Nalasis leaders suggested that Teva came and collected all the slit-gongs and took them away if they were theirs. This did not suit Teva, as the point was not that they wanted the slit-gongs (rather they wanted the money the slit-gongs were to generate in the particular trajectory imagined for them). Edward repeated the threat Nalsen had made in the previous dispute, that he would leave the land, the slit-gongs and all the items of *kastom* Wamu had received from Sombee (*tse'sopung, kaapu, hokung*) to go back into the hands of Teva. But in return he would revoke all Serieng's use of such intangibles which had their origin in Reite *palems*, and which they shared with Reite. Claiming he was not cross, but only wanting to avoid future complaints over things he knew he owned, he proposed the radical solution of the severance of long-standing shared productions. This suggestion was met with real horror by all the senior people present. It was tantamount to revoking the kinship connections of many generations.

It took a leader who was not of either Serieng or Nalasis to divert the issue away from the anger between the parties, and break several hours of stalemate. He explained that I was not actually purchasing the slit-gongs. I was paying for people's work on one slit-gong, which was not to be sold, but put in a museum. The butchered pigs waiting to be cooked were payment made to the spiritual powers that aided in the construction of the drums, and when the community ate these, the payment would be finished. This apparently got to the heart of the matter for Teva people. An apparent aside in the main dispute over land, trees and history proved to be central to the issue as Teva saw it.

Teva were surprised and angered by the suggestion that the connections of previous generations would be severed over the claim they were making. The phrases used were that 'cross-cousin and grandparents would be finished between them' and they would 'live broken apart', should the shared use of items of *kastom* and intangible forms of self-production be terminated. It appeared that Teva and Serieng people more generally were not ready to let this happen, and considered it an overreaction by Nalasis to the claim that was being made.

Exegesis

The heat of the exchange resulted in a strength of response which the Teva complainants had not expected.[13] For them the issue was the new productive relations in which Nalasis appeared engaged. These relations had at their base a place of common origin, a shared nexus in the ongoing relations between Teva and Nalasis. Ownership of *kastom* items, such as *tse'sopung*, are justified, and *valued*, because of where they have come from. Differentiation between the identity of neighbours, or of siblings descended from a single *palem*, are made by the particular forms of *kastom* they have in common with their (different) affines. *Palem* are defined and generated in their relations with affines, and each *palem* has a different configuration of affinal relations. It is this unique configuration of relations with affines that allows the generation of new *palem* without necessarily severing the siblingship ties people have through common origin in a historically distant *palem*.[14] Thus within the overarching name of Ripia the members of distinct *palem*s think of themselves as siblings with other Ripia people. Ripia is the origin of Nalasis *palem*, Putputkin *palem* and Saruk *palem*. Each named entity uses different *kastom* – designs and tunes – when they make affinal payments. These different forms of *kastom* make reference to their parents and grandparents affinal relations, whereby those smaller groupings of Ripia (Nalasis, Putputkin, Saruk) came into being as distinct places.

As I outlined above, making an affinal payment is the way that corporation is demonstrated among those people resident in an particular named place (and see Wagner 1967 for a seminal anthropological account from elsewhere in PNG). They remember their overarching origin (Ripia) and siblingship though it, but become known as an entity in their own right, named after the land on which they made their affinal payment (Nalasis, Saruk etc.). Because each marriage is likely to generate new affinal relations, each *palem* is constituted *as such* by different relations to those of its sibling *palem*s within an overarching name.

It was the catalogue of a significant and impressive collection of highly valued forms or designs (*kaapu, hokung, tse'sopung*) which was brought to bear as a clinching argument in the case of this dispute. These forms are closely identified with the place and people who created them, and are jealously guarded against use or imitation by other *palem*. They figure in the work of production and reproduction, as gardens must have *hokung* (plantings) at their centre to encourage taro to grow, *kaapu* (spirits) grow children in the womb of their mothers, and grow adolescents into adults during initiations. As the growth of children and their transformation into adults comes about through the particular power of *a specific* design or spirit, not through the general power of spirits, growth itself is dependent upon particular affinal connections. Then again, at the moment that a *palem* demonstrates its productiveness in wealth and children during an affinal payment, it makes these obligations apparent once more by displaying the designs and tunes shared with previous affinal relations, as the marker of its own identity. It is the reference to where things have come from that justifies use. And *palem* identity is demonstrated by producing items which embody the memory of its multiple relational origins.

Use of particular *tse'sopung* designs by the descendants of Wamu are not shared by all Nalasis people. Thus when Edward made a *palem* on the site of Nalasis, he could differentiate himself and his particular identity through the use of designs which referred to the productive relations his ancestor Wamu had in the past with his affines. Power to achieve such differentiation, and therefore visibility as a *palem* head in one's own right, is wrapped up in relations to *palem* ancestors' maternal kin.

Tse'sopung such as *kau sareining* facilitate the attraction of members of other *palem* to one's lands, desire to enter exchange relations with the producers, and even attract women to marry into the *palem* that display them. In this case, the fact that these powerful and valuable forms had come from elsewhere (marriage between Tapuwang and Nalasis *palem*) bound the identity of certain members of Nalasis *palem* to their previous constitutive relations with Teva.

Notice that when pressed by continuing dispute, the magistrate said that it was not the land that was at issue. Rather, he wanted to focus on the things produced by that land. Thus the claim was over the slit-gongs. But then Teva were not interested in taking the slit-gongs as compensation. In fact, the claim was over the relations with others which the slit-gongs were supposed to facilitate. Production involves obligation and relationships. Some of the success of this production of slit-gongs could be traced, according to Teva, to the land on which the tree was grown. This in turn spoke of a shared history and interdependent identity between the two *palem*. How were relationships to be reconciled? Where did Teva fit in the perceived breakthrough made by Nalasis people in generating a large amount of wealth, especially as it occurred at the nexus between the two *palem*. That these kinds of questions were the background to the dispute explains both the timing of the letter (the slit-gongs had been successfully produced and were in the process of facilitating wealth exchanges); and the fact that the land itself was not the resource claimed. It was not even the things produced that were of interest to Teva people in the case of the second dispute. And notice that the claims to regain the land in the first dispute came only once it appeared to be essential to the construction of a road for Reite, who would not be diverted from their intention (i.e. recognise Teva's connection). What can easily appear as destructive impediments to development because of local jealousy, have a more complex origin.

The two claims focussed on transactions where access to wealth and power in the wider world were apparently to be achieved by one group of people who shared a constitutive history with another, made concrete in certain shared things. The particular piece of land involved was one of these things. Payments made for the slit-gongs were likely to be divided among all who could claim support for, or work on, the project. The stimulation of my desire to possess slit-gongs might well have made those that constructed them think of the source of their own power and identity in the very history of relations which the land at <u>Posondaring</u> and <u>Isik Guhung</u> bore testimony to. In fact, Teva could make some claim over Edward himself, as the descendant of Wamu, whose name and recognition had been provided in large part by his affines, and particularly Sombee. Kinship terms between the disputants bore testimony to this continuing connection and obligation. If Edward was to carry forward the value of this joint production into the future, then should there not be reference made, through distribution of the outcome of the transaction (wealth), to the source of its value?

Two factors made the claim inadmissible. Firstly, once it was clear that overall recognition for the slit-gong manufacture was not to come in the form of substantial wealth which could then be redistributed along the paths made by the history of relations, the claim itself dissipated. This is significant, as the payment for the slit-gongs would appear (without ethnographic contextualisation) to be external to the actual issue behind the complaint (land ownership). Secondly, reference to the unspecified 'services rendered' reminded the claimants that land may well have been legitimately passed between the *palem*. Hence the argument became focussed on the products, and the uses to which those products were to be put. The issue was not then the legitimacy of the manufacture any more, but how boundaries were to be drawn in relation to who was to benefit from 'development'.

Nekgini speakers have complex and highly developed mechanisms for finishing ongoing claims generated in the context of affinal relations. There are twelve separate payments made by a male child to his maternal kin, prior to marriage, for example. Each one removes one of the highly articulated and differentiated obligations he has to them (first decoration, first consumption of meat, initiation, etc.) for his emergence as an effective social entity. Some young people in these villages say that these obligations, entailed 'in' *kastom*, are too onerous. They are not interested in them. Yet it is in these transactions that knowledge of obligation and value generation is developed. In both resolutions, it was the revelation of such knowledge that dissipated ignorant claims. Since my departure, there has been no renewal of claims over <u>Posondaring</u> and <u>Isik Guhung</u>. Edward has left them (perhaps sensibly) as areas of bush, rather than planting cash crops on them.

Conclusion

On revisiting these disputes with Edward in 1999, he told me that in the case of the slit-gong dispute, Teva subsequently apologised, explaining that it was not their wish to come and complain, but that someone had been inciting them to anger[15] with talk of how much money Nalasis would make from producing slit-gongs on their land. This brings us back to my initial point about drawing boundaries to one's obligations. The man who had been inciting Teva to anger, I realised, was someone I had overlooked in the process of making the collection of contemporary objects.

Bounding obligations is integral to the process of commodification, with the state and its laws determining the scope of admissible claims. The notion of resource, as Edwardo Viveiros de Castro recently articulated (personal communication) is premised on a notion of scarcity. Perceived scarcity incites people to bound the use of things, limiting access to them. People's identity becomes linked to control over resources or property. These people are protected by the rights they hold in law over their property. The state guarantees laws are upheld.

In the ethnography I have presented here, it is clear that no one object was the focus of dispute. The resource was not the land in question. It was transactions involving land, in both cases, which called forth ramifying connections and which placed the value of the current transaction in a context of other productive relations, that is other transactions. The resource, if one can call it that, was the history of kinship, placement and identity as a process of production. The burden of my analysis is that this kind of understanding of the value of land does not allow that its legitimate connection to one set of people comes wholly at the expense of other people.

Yet this is exactly what the model of corporate groups connected through exclusive substance passed on at conception, and whose identity is bound up with the control of certain property (land) as resource, achieves. In Nekgini practice, land comes to be of significance as a site upon which relations have been productive. The identity of those using this land is dependent upon the continued reference they make to their relationships with others. In this chapter then I have provided concrete examples of how *kastom*, history, kinship and identity appear in people's rationales for ownership.

Notes

1. I gratefully acknowledge the support of the Leverhulme Trust and the Newton Trust for their financial support while this article was written, and of the ESRC who funded the field research. My sincere thanks go also to the people of Reite and Sarangama villages, to the NRI in Port Moresby, and to Madang Provincial Government for permission to undertake research in the Province. Don Niles provided support and encouragement during the events recounted at one point in this chapter which I remember with gratitude.

2. In this chapter, as elsewhere, I refer to people from these villages as 'Nekgini speaking people'. This I mean to stand as short-hand for 'Nekgini speaking people whom I know, and are happy for me to represent their opinions and perceptions as a coherent body of understanding'.

3. See below (Background: Social Organisation and Land), for the explanation as to why male ancestors are remembered more readily than female ones, without reference to notions of succession and inheritance based on biogenetic inheritance.

4. Based on observations made by Nekgini people, and related to me, on schemes to collect genealogical information because of the approach of the Ramu Nickel project during 1999.

5. For clarity, I retain the use of *italics* for the vernacular and for Tok Pisin terms throughout. Place names and land names are <u>underlined</u>. Unmarked proper nouns are people's names, and group names.

6. The identification between fathers and sons does not involve the transmission of an essence at conception, but rather the nurturant properties of the land that are brought to bear, through the work of the father and his kin, on the child. It is this *situated* or placed work which generates identification, in the name of that place.

7. Payment perhaps for sorcery work, or other activities such as knowledge transmission that would not have been made public.

8. 'After 1904, each village or hamlet cluster was placed under a native headman or luluai ... who had to maintain order, guard the village census book, report epidemics, and settle minor disputes.' (Lawrence 1964: 42–3).

9. Roads in Fuyuge are 'an idiom for denoting social action and agency' according to Hirsch.

10. I thank Mark Busse and Michael O'Hanlon for their help with this project.

11. Those interested in this process will find it documented in the article 'Drum and Voice' (Leach 2002).

12. 'Mipela i no wari long wanem ol tok promis ol man i dai pinis bin mekim. Mipela bai no inup harim toktok bilong yupela. Mipela harim yupela wokim ol garamut long groun bilong mipela. Mipela harim olsem yu wokim etpela garamut. Mipela laikim yupela mus baim ol disela garamut nau tasol.'

13. Although they might have been expected to do so. In what follows, I make a stab at contextualising what appeared to me at the time as a simple issue of land ownership. Either Nalasis did own the land, and the Teva complaint collapsed, or they did not, which put Nalasis firmly in the wrong. My allegiances being what they were, I viewed the Teva complaint as opportunistic at best. My analysis here, which some might say makes the Teva complaint look reasonable given the facts they had been given (see below), comes from consideration of the particular way in which any transaction is embedded in other transactions among Nekgini speakers. Making things intelligible in this anthropological mode is not to detract from the genuine anger exhibited at the meeting. Like the transactions, contextualisation is never complete. Additional elements which might be relevant here are the fact that in the three months of slit-gong construction, no complaint had been voiced by Teva. Waiting until their emergence rather cornered Edward. It was also at a time of ceremonial activity, when the spirits of the male cult were present in the village. It is just unacceptable to disturb people during the time they are in concert with powerful spirits and ancestors. Perhaps this was part of the background to Edward's anger.

14. Except of course in the case where, as often happens, people marry 'siblings'. This turns residual siblingship because of common origin in a particular *palem*, into relations of exchange appropriate between affines.
15. 'Sutim bel' in Tok Pisin. The abdomen is thought of as the site of emotion by Nekgini speakers, and this phrase evokes the way anger is stirred in the belly through malicious talk which incites jealousy.

5

The Bases of Ownership Claims Over Natural Resources by Indigenous Peoples in Papua New Guinea

Lawrence Kalinoe

Marilyn Strathern recently made the following observations, which in my view beautifully capture the age old desire of human kind to make ownership claims over the parts of the natural environment that they live in. These observations in many ways also resonate with the age old desire, perhaps fantasy, of humankind to keep on looking out for that particular part of nature which may give one wealth and riches some day. Of Euro-American moderns Strathern observes:

> [People] become attached to a world they see full of useful and beautiful things. It is a world that they imagine that people desire to appropriate, whether they think of private individuals in exclusive possession of property or of the common people in open possession of its bounty. Ownership. What is not owned exists either to be owned as some future resource not yet exploited or else is notionally owned by humankind in general, including generations to come. Ownership envelops all (2001: 12).

There are a number of models by which people appropriate part or parts of nature, particularly those 'useful and beautiful things', to make them their 'own'. One model is that of John Locke, in which the application of labour to such things appropriates them; another model is based on inheriting, or otherwise acquiring them through relationships, as is the case among many indigenous peoples of the Pacific and the Americas. In fact, 'ownership' is the essence of property rights in all types of human societies; regardless of whether, employing Honore's dichotomy, those societies 'exist in "mature legal systems" or "primitive systems", such as that of the Trobriand Islanders.' (1961: 106). In one sense, 'ownership' also refers to property itself (Tyler and Palmer 1973: 3): 'the bundles of mutual rights and obligations which prevail between "subjects" [people] in respect of certain "objects" [things]' which they "own" (Gray: 1987: 9).

It must also be stated at the outset that the Lockean route to 'ownership' (the fruit of labour metaphor; the application of one's labour to make that thing the labourer's) and then turning those 'useful and beautiful things' into property is not the most common route to 'ownership' and hence property in the customary legal order in Papua New Guinea, or most indigenous societies for that matter. Rather, relationships in terms of how one relates to those 'useful and beautiful things', be they subject–object relationships or subject–subject relationships, are the predominant route to 'ownership'. It is this which in many instances translates into property rights. Relationship, in all sorts of forms or variations, is the dominant route to ownership, rather than labour. The reference to 'subject–subject' relationship here refers to one's relations, either vertically (that is in the sense of being intergenerational) or horizontally (within the same generation), where ownership rights are claimed and exercised by members of lineages, clans or other such social groups in a given society. For instance, in customary land tenure that exists in parts of Papua New Guinea, tracing genealogy to an apical ancestor within relevant totemic cosmologies forms the basis of land tenure and gives 'ownership' to customary land. Perhaps only in limited circumstances, labour, through the doctrine of adverse possession, may with the passage of time, give ownership: see Amet J's (as he then was)[1] decision in *Re Hides Gas Land Case* [1993] PNGLR 309. In fact, when one takes a moment to think about ownership claims and property rights in indigenous Papua New Guinea, it becomes obvious that it is really the 'subject–subject' relationship in the first instance that gives one ownership claims and such other rights to access and use natural resources. The 'subject–object' relationship is really one that is supposed to exist between an institution, such as a clan (as 'owners'), and the natural resources in question, rather than the individual members that make up the clan, lineage etc. Hence the 'subject–object' becomes blurry whereas the 'subject–subject' relationship becomes more visual and real.

The desire to appropriate those 'useful and beautiful things' is nowadays not only found in the affluent countries of the West, but is also in so called Indigenous societies (but perhaps at a reduced scale). With particular reference to natural resources in those so called Indigenous states, Papua New Guinea being one of them, the claims of ownership are invariably based on a number of things. The main one is the relationship that one has, or stands with, relative to the land upon which those 'useful and beautiful things' are found; others, like the relationship that the claimant has with the relevant totemic cosmologies etc., pertain to the metaphysical origins of the 'useful and beautiful' items concerned. One thing is therefore clear, if a person cannot point to such relationships, particularly in Papua New Guinea, then one's claim to those 'useful and beautiful things' is clearly based on shifting sand and cannot hold.

This chapter begins by looking at the concept of 'ownership' and 'possession' in common law and then examines how these concepts may relate, or indeed relate to, customary land tenure law in Papua New Guinea. It does so by looking at Amet J's decision in *The Re Hides Gas Land Case* [1993] PNGLR 309 and also generally considers the implications of this decision for other natural resources, particularly customary water use rights. The bases of ownership claims of customary water resources are also considered.

The Concept of Ownership

Ownership of course underpins property: that is, apart from the technical distinction in law between ownership and title, ownership is the platform upon which property rights are claimed. Ownership accords property rights to a person (including legal persons or the person as a corporate entity) or persons by first excluding other claimants from the object being claimed. Prohibitive norms that regulate human activities (such as laws in the so-called mature legal systems or customary laws in the so-called primitive systems, now known as Indigenous systems) and human conduct towards the object claimed (as property) then gives ownership its peculiar attributes: exclusiveness of use, possession, or management of the object; rights of undisturbed enjoyment; and its transmissibility, i.e., the right to dispose of the thing as and when necessary. Whilst prohibitive norms secure ownership in the first place, the existence of normative orders (normal or acceptable behaviour or conduct) in a given society also acts as restraint on others so that they do not interfere with the owner's enjoyment of property. In many societies today, statute laws also protect ownership rights, invariably with sanctions. But from the standpoint of the 'owner', legal systems or such other normative orders give the owner subjective rights to enjoy or deal otherwise with the property. Ownership rights are however not absolute and the following passage from Turner articulates this:

The law of ownership is not a set of rules fixing what I may or may not do to a thing but a set of rules fixing what other people may or may not prevent me from doing to the thing, and what I may or may not prevent them from doing to the thing (1941: 343).

Indeed, particularly in these days, town planning and environmental legislation and the law of nuisance (common law) do, in a real way, indirectly impose constraints on the exercise of ownership rights in the sense that one's exercise of property rights should not interfere with the rights of others.

Particularly in the ownership of land (excluding customary land), it is important to point out that one does not own the land as an object, but rather the rights (bundle of rights) to secured access, use and enjoyment for a determinable, usually long-term, period. These rights and privilege are obtained through a document called the title deed, either as a lease or, until Independence (1975), a freehold tenure. Ownership of the land, that is the radical title, is always with the Crown, now the State by virtue of the power of dominion. For instance, when a person in Papua New Guinea says that they are buying land from the State (Government), that person is actually buying the rights and privileges associated with the use of the land from the State because what that person obtains is a State lease for (say the maximum period of) 99 years rather than the land itself as an object. In this instance, therefore, it is proper to speak of 'title' rather than ownership. And, as generally in the common law tradition, disputes over rights of exclusive use and enjoyment and disposal of such land are usually settled through the search for a 'better title' to the land rather than through asking questions of 'ownership'. Although there are no 'title deeds' in customary land tenure in Papua New Guinea, the general concept that individual members of, say, a landowning clan or lineage have use rights only, and that the ownership of the land is vested in the clan or lineage, is very similar to the land tenure system concerning State leases. So even in this instance, the individual member does not own the land as an object, but rather obtains and exercises access, use and enjoyment rights over that piece of customary land from the institution or lineage that they belong to (clan etc.,) who owns the land.

The assertion made earlier that ownership claims and indeed ownership of customary land in Papua New Guinea, are made by establishing relationships – either 'subject–object' or 'subject–subject' relationships – is clearly demonstrated when one considers the range of evidence a party to a dispute over customary land before the Local and District Land Courts, the Land Titles Commission or the National Court, has to adduce to make out its case. The courts in Papua New Guinea have called this kind of evidence, traditional evidence. The pre-independence case of *Administration of Papua New Guinea v Guba Doriga* [1973] ALJR 621 is one of the first court cases involving traditional evidence.

This case involved a dispute over the declaration and application of the common law land law doctrine of waste and vacant (*bona vacantia*) to land in the Territory of Papua, particularly customary land that the Administration is alleged to have acquired through this process, and the admission of traditional evidence into evidence by the customary landowners that these lands were not waste and vacant, but were actually owned and used by the indigenous Motuan people. In coming to terms with what traditional evidence entails, Barwick CJ of the High Court of Australia, said at p. 635:

> By traditional evidence, I understand [that to be] the statement of a witness who claims either to have been the repository of folklore of a primitive community or to have been told relevant facts by some of his fore fathers who had an important place in that community, standing which was likely to have made them knowledgeable in the relevant aspects.

Then in the post-independence National Court decision in *Re Fishermen Island Case* [1979] PNGLR 202, Wilson J considered traditional evidence (at p. 208) to encompass 'rights existing beyond living memory which may be admitted to prove title particularly title to family land whose oral evidence are the only evidence available.' Traditional evidence is therefore largely oral evidence that is usually based around genealogy, oral history, legends and mythology and sometimes may involve cultural artefacts and explanation of their significance, customs, territory, and boundary marks of family land etc.

In both these cases cited above (and those not further cited like *Madana Resena v Papua New Guinea* [1990] PNGLR), to stake out their ownership claims the parties had to adduce the following type of traditional evidence: genealogies tracing to the apical ancestor that first arrived on the land and or used the land and the subsequent history of succession and divestiture, either through intertribal warfare or natural attrition of the landowning lineage; the name of that ancestor or ancestors; the land use patterns or marks left behind by that ancestor and the parties' ability to point to and identify remains of such land use marks, like for example the place at which they made their houses, fire places (*sit paia* in Pidgin), garden land characterised by plots, mounds or drainage systems and such other plants of significance left behind such as economic trees (breadfruit trees, *karuka* palm trees, sago palms, various species of palms used for house building etc.) and ceremonial plants ('tanget', hibiscus, 'crotons' etc.); knowledge of the natural landscape of the land area under dispute and perhaps the cosmologies associated with some mountain ridges, names of the mountain ridges and valleys, creeks, streams, lakes or rivers flowing through the area and of course the associated cosmologies and whether the claimants have any spiritual, ritual or magico-religious connections to the mountains, valleys, streams, creeks, lakes, rivers etc. Consequently, I have elsewhere made the observation that:

> Customary landownership in Papua New Guinea and in most indigenous societies of the world is extensively intertwined with traditional legend and cosmology passed down from the earlier generation to the next. In this intricate equation, genealogy tracing prior occupation and life of ancestors lost in defending that particular land clearly stands to be the leading and paramount factors in determining the ownership of customary land'(Kalinoe 1993: 8).

Now if we take time to dissect the kind of evidence that claimants to customary land are required to adduce to make out their respective cases, it becomes obvious that it all hinges on relationships, in whatever shape or form. That is, how the claimants relate to 'things' on the land (knowledge of plants/trees, mountains ridges, caves, creeks) at the 'subject–object' level. At the 'subject–subject' level, you find evidence of genealogies, the names of ancestors lost in intertribal attacks when defending the land in dispute or such other resources on the land; relationship to the ancestor that, say, made the garden or planted the palm tree; relationship to the first person that walked on the land and/or dead ancestors buried on the land. Hence, Strathern (although she is particularly referring to the *kamals,* the landowning unit on Ponam Island, Manus Province) reads the situation well and aptly captures it (for the whole of Papua New Guinea and not only for Ponam Islanders), when she says: 'land is held through numerous transactions which link persons to numerous others; among these others is also a group that lays title to it' (1998a: 141).

At this juncture, it is also worthwhile to state briefly the concepts of 'beneficial owner' and 'legal owner', where the latter, as trustee, holds property on trust for the former (the beneficial owner) under the common law and equity principles found in the law of trust. The trustee as the legal owner is entitled to exercise all rights of ownership over the particular property held on trust, but the exercise of ownership rights must always be in the interest of the beneficial owner, not in the self-interest of the legal owner. Hence, 'realistically, beneficial ownership is of a more substantial nature. The beneficiary may in appropriate circumstances affect the disposition of the trust property by his consent thereto; he may enter into arrangements with the others interested beneficially in the trust property, to the effect of overriding the terms of the trust.' (Tyler and Palmer 1973: 44).

Now, how do we relate these principles to customary land tenure in Papua New Guinea? Do these principles have value and stand to make a contribution towards the future development of the principles of customary land tenure so that disputes within the landowning customary group are amicably settled, preventing such disputes from escalating and posing a threat to the very institution of customary land tenure itself? I would like to think that they do. And with the guidance provided by these well tried principles of common law which have withstood time, together with related or similar concepts offered by customary law on customary land tenure, the courts in Papua New Guinea, in an appropriate case, can develop a similar principle of underlying law. This can go a long way towards strengthening the institution of customary land tenure which, in recent times, particularly with the introduction of the long-term cash crop economy, is experiencing some stress.

Preliminary results of a recent survey (carried out by Kalinoe and Muroa, 1999–2000) indicate that the use of customary land by other members of the customary landowning group for long-term cash cropping, like coconut plantations, cocoa plantations and coffee plantations, is denying the other members of the landowning group use of the land to which, as customary landowners, they all have equal rights. This is causing some tension amongst the same landowning group members. Now, if one is to look at this emerging situation along the lines of the trust law concepts of 'beneficial ownership' and 'legal ownership', the following argument can be plausibly raised. Those so called 'customary landowners' who build coconut, cocoa, and coffee plantations on customary land must realise that they do not personally 'own' the land but are, really, self-appointed trustees, who as legal owners hold the land for the time being for the beneficial owners, who are the unborn and the dead, and therefore they have no right to deny others from making beneficial use of the same land.

Possession

Whilst ownership and possession are very much intertwined and therefore appear to rest on one another, they are however distinct concepts. Let me illustrate this: Z owns a house boat but is not living in it now and therefore has got Q to live in it. So Q now has possession and enjoyment of the houseboat (either on lease or on hire), but he knows and accepts that he does not own it. Ownership is with Z.

In many instances however, possession is said to be the 'prima facie proof of ownership' (Tyler and Palmer 1973: 45) and it is up to the other side to disprove ownership. In disputes over ownership, possession gives the possessor a strong presumption of ownership (see *The Hides Gas Land Case* [1993] PNGLR 309).

Uninterrupted adverse possession, over a passage of time, may mature into 'ownership' or legally enforceable property rights. Particularly with customary land tenure, Amet J decided exactly this in the Re Hides Gas Land Case, when he, in all instances, awarded ownership of various disputed customary land to those clans and/or tribes, or even some clans only from the main tribe, who were physically in possession, as opposed to those who were not, despite whatever convincing evidence they produced to stake out their claims. At p.319 of his judgement, this is what Amet J said:

> Applying all these principles to the factual circumstances, which principally involve the Tuguba Tribe on the one side and the Hiwa tribe clans on the other, the overwhelming preponderance of evidence and equity weigh towards the incumbent occupants against those who are not in physical occupation on the land... All of these principles weigh in favour of the Kopiye against the Yugu Tuguba Pate and the Ware in respect of the campsite and water line easement. In respect of all other land, they weigh in favour of all Hiwa clans who are on the land against all the complainant Tuguba Tribe clans.

Apart from the case that possession is a significant factor or aspect of ownership, the common law has always treated possession to constitute three main distinct elements: (a) the fact of physical control, detention – otherwise known as de facto possession; (b) legal possession that can be recognised and protected by law; and (c) the right to have either legal or physical possession (see Tyler and Palmer 1973: 47). The main distinction of consequence in law between these three instances of possession is that possession alone as in (a) or the right to possession only as in (c), are of no legal significance in that no legally enforceable rights arise, whereas legal possession as in (b) involves possession capable of recognition, and hence enforced by law. Inherent in this category of possession (legal possession) is 'animus possedendi, the intention to hold the thing against others.' (Stewart and Burgess 1996: 303). Tyler and Palmer (1973: 49), usefully describe 'legal possession' in these terms:

> Here we have a definite legal relation but one which may exist without physical control or without lawful origin. The person who has both title to and physical control of a chattel has, of course, legal possession, but so also has he who has physical control of and a manifest intention to exercise a dominion over a chattel ... legal possession may exist in the absence of physical control, as where a man's goods are in the hands of his servant.

With regard to category (c) possession – the right to have either physical or legal possession as referred to above, Tyler and Palmer explain that this arises when a person has lost either legal or physical possession of their property, either by agreement (e.g., as in a bailment situation) or through theft or conversion; the person is left with rights either to legal possession or physical possession, and these rights may perhaps materialise some time in the future. 'Or it may be the right of one who is entitled but has never obtained possession, as in the case of the purchaser who has paid the price of goods bought but has not had delivery thereof.' (1973: 50).

The following (two) common law cases are cited to illustrate, first (the first case) the kind of situation that may constitute legal possession, and second (the second case) the kind of situation that may not. The first case is *The Tubantia* [1924] P. 78, involving rival salvage operators confronting each other in a salvage operation to salvage the cargo of the vessel *Tubantia*, a Dutch steamer that sank in the North Sea in waters of up to 100 feet. The plaintiffs had successfully salvaged the vessel and were in the process of recovering the cargo, when the defendants, who were also pursuing the same shipwreck disturbed them. The plaintiffs successfully sued the defendants for trespassing and obtained an injunction against the defendants. Damages were also awarded to the plaintiffs. In coming to arrive at his decision, the judge Sir Henry Duke P, first raised the following issues:

> What are the kinds of physical control and use of which the things in question were practically capable? Could physical control be applied to the *res* as a whole? Was there a complete taking? Had the plaintiffs occupation sufficient for practical purposes to exclude strangers from interfering with the property? Was there the *animus possidendi*?

His Honour then deliberated:

> There was *animus possidendi* in the plaintiffs. There was the use and occupation of which the subject matter was capable. There was power to exclude strangers from interfering if the plaintiffs did not use unlawful force. The plaintiff did with the wreck what a purchaser would prudently have done. Unwieldy as the wreck was, they were dealing with it as a whole. The fact on the other side which is outstanding is the difficulty of possessing things which lie in very deep water and can only be entered upon by workmen in fine weather and for short periods of time. Must it be said that, because the work of the plaintiffs' was that of only one pair at a time, in short spells with long interruptions, and because access to the holds of the *Tubantia* was often prevented altogether by stress of weather, therefore the vessel, and her cargo were incapable of possession? To my mind this would be an unfortunate conclusion ... and I do not feel bound to come to it. I hold that the plaintiffs had in July, 1923, the possession of the *Tubantia* and her cargo, which they allege.

In the second case of *Young v Hichens* (1834) 6 Q.B. 606, the plaintiff was fishing for pilchards and was in the process of gathering the fish into his net when the defendant disturbed him by rowing his boat into the opening of the net. The defendant's action of course disturbed the fish, and hence denied the plaintiff from catching (capturing) the pilchards. The plaintiff then sued the defendant for trespass and sought damages. In refusing judgement for the plaintiff, this is what Lord Denman C.J. said:

> It does appear almost certain that the plaintiff would have had possession of the fish but for the act of the defendant: but it is quite certain that he had not possession. Whatever interpretation may be put on such terms as 'custody' and 'possession', the question will be whether any custody or possession has been obtained here. I think it [is] impossible to say that it had, until the party had actual power over the fish. It may be that the defendant acted unjustifiably in preventing the plaintiff from obtaining such power: but that would only show a wrongful act, for which he might be liable in a proper form of action.

Ownership Claims Over Natural Resources in Papua New Guinea

There is no doubt that the ownership of customary land is the basis of many of the claims to natural resources that Indigenous Papua New Guineans are making. Hence, since that is the case, let us now look at, albeit briefly, some of the main features of land law and customary land tenure against the background of the concept of ownership as briefly considered above.

Land policy in Papua New Guinea since the colonial administration, has always recognised, preserved and even protected, customary land tenure. Hence customary landowners continue to hold or own land under customary law. Various land law legislation, since the colonial period, has always recognised, protected, and preserved customary land tenure, largely by prohibiting all dealings in customary land without prior consent from the State: see Section 4 of the *Land Act* 1996. Even the State itself is required to purchase land from customary landowners if it requires land for State use or developmental projects. In instances where the customary landowners refuse to sell customary land, provided the proposed land use by the State is in the 'national interest', the State is given power of 'compulsory acquisition'. But then again, such powers are considerably curtailed by the operation of Section 53 of the *Constitution* (of Papua New Guinea) which constitutionally legislates against the unjust deprivation or appropriation of property by the State and its agencies. Section 53 of the Constitution provides that, except in the specific circumstances allowed by the Constitution itself, such as compulsory acquisition of land for 'public purpose' (in the national interest), the government or such other public authority must not compulsorily take 'property' or 'interest in or rights over property' without compensation on just terms. So in the Papua New Guinea situation, the fact of dominion by the State over the country does not at all vest all land in the State as in many other Commonwealth jurisdictions, but instead legitimises and consolidates customary land tenure, wholly regulated by customary law. If I may be allowed to digress from the topic at hand, this is really (at least to me) the irony of the pre-Mabo *'terra nullius'* position in Australia: while the Australians, as the colonial power, were protecting customary land tenure and customary law in their then Territory of Papua and New Guinea, they denied the same at home for nearly two hundred years, until judicial intervention by the High Court in the so called landmark decision in *Mabo (No 2)* (1992) 107 ALR 1.

Lea (1994: 117), in looking at the philosophy of customary land tenure in Melanesia, argues that, philosophically considered, customary land tenure does not give 'fully blown' property rights and therefore is not a jural reality. I beg to differ on the basis that when a legislature of competent jurisdiction passes laws and gives the subject matter legal effect, that automatically becomes a jural reality within that jurisdiction, and that is exactly the case in Papua New Guinea.

Even so, customary land tenure, initially through the existence of normative orders in the respective societies in which it prevails, and subsequently sanctioned by State laws, has always had features of property rights, in particular 'ownership' such that the holders of customary land have always had and continue to exercise rights of exclusivity over its use and enjoyment (admittedly with very limited and restricted rights of disposal). But should that (limited disposal rights) disqualify customary land tenure as a non-proprietary right or a lesser property right? No. Particularly not when laws have made customary land tenure a recognised property right as is the case in Papua New Guinea.

In land law within common law and statute law, land has a very broad meaning and includes both 'corporeal hereditaments' and 'incorporeal hereditaments', where generally the former refers to physical improvements or chattels on the land and the latter refers to the intangible rights that inhere in the use and enjoyment of the land. Gray explains these two concepts well, with appropriate illustrations, when he says, first of 'corporeal hereditaments':

Corporeal hereditaments comprise those substantial and permanent objects which affect the senses, the only objects which are truly permanent being those constituted by or connected with immovable property. In the extended sense..., corporeal hereditaments include not merely the physical clods of earth which make up the surface layer of land, but also all physical things which are attached to or are inherent in the ground. Thus the term ... comprehends such things as buildings, trees and subjacent minerals (1987: 16, footnotes omitted).

And then of 'incorporeal hereditaments':

In contradistinction to 'corporeal hereditaments' which are tangible, incorporeal hereditaments are not the object of sensation, can neither be seen nor handled, are creatures of the mind, and exist only in contemplation. An important modern example of this category of intangible rights is the right of way which one landowner, A, may have over the land of another, B (1987: 38, footnotes omitted).

This very wide import given to the meaning of land has been with us since the medieval (13th century) common law Latin maxim: *cuius est solum eius est usquead coelum et ad infernos*, meaning: he who owns the land owns everything reaching up to the very heavens and down to the depths of the earth. Of course, these days, this maxim cannot be literally taken as accurately stating the law for the reason that other principles of law, such as the Crown dominion over royal minerals at common law and other statutory rules such as the conservation management principles under the *Conservation Areas Act* have negated this *cuius est solum* maxim. Ownership rights over minerals and hydrocarbons (oil, natural gas, coal etc.,) are usually vested by legislation on the State rather than the landowner. For example, in Papua New Guinea the *Mining Act 1992* and the *Petroleum Act Chapter 198* (Revised Laws of PNG) vests ownership rights on the State regardless of where these minerals and hydrocarbons are found: on State land or on customary land.

Except for water in tidal rivers, the common law also regards non-tidal inland watercourses (rivers, streams or lakes) as a 'species of land' and 'regard such areas of water as simply areas of land covered with water' (Gray 1987: 31) and the landowner may have exclusive rights of fishery because 'fisheries are in their nature mere profits of the soil over which the water flows, and that the title to a fishery arises from the right to the solum', *Attorney General for British Columbia v Attorney General for Canada* [1914] AC 153 at 167.

Common law also includes trees, plants and flowers with the meaning of land for they comprise part of the land which they are found growing on, whether in the wild or cultivated and therefore become 'part of the estate owned by the landowner' (Gray 1987: 25).

With regard to the ownership of airspace as part of the land, in reality this is commonly associated with the lower stratum of the airspace rather than the higher stratum (reaching up to the very heavens). In this regard, Gray (1987: 26) says: 'There is no doubt that the rights of the owner extend to limited portions of airspace both above and below the ground level within those physical geographical boundaries'.

These common law principles concerning the meaning of, or rather the attributes of, land are very similar to how Indigenous Papua New Guineans view land, customary land in particular. Since it is from the land that they eke out their livelihood, it is therefore very obvious that land to them include the trees, the forest, the flora and fauna, the rivers, the lakes, the seas, the fish in them, the sago, their gardens and 'all those useful and beautiful things' and those not so useful and beautiful things found on their land. With particular reference to the 'ownership' of a river or parts of a river by the respective customary landowners, I refer to the following exchange between myself and an emotionally charged village elder of Iniok village, a village situated on the banks of the upper Sepik River and about one kilometre downstream from the mouth of the Freida River that empties into the Sepik. This exchange took place in early February of 1996:

> In the village of Iniok, an elder went to the extent of asking me whether the river or parts of the river, lake or stream were hanging from thin air? When I replied no, he explained that the land holds the water and determines its course and direction of flow. And that land through which the river, lake or stream flows is of course owned by a clan or tribe and therefore, by virtue of the ownership of the land, that clan or tribe owns that particular watercourse(Kalinoe 1999: 209).

Ownership claims over natural resources by Indigenous Papua New Guineans are therefore made on the bases of the ownership of customary land, or rather more accurately, on the basis of the relationship that they have with the clan, lineage or such other social grouping that they belong to which, in effect, owns customary land.

Possession and Ownership of Customary Land: Re Hides Gas Land Case

In the case of *Re Hides Gas Project Land Case* [1993] PNGLR 309, a series of disputes arose amongst several customary landowning clans of two main tribes who were each claiming ownership of the land on which the Hides Gas Project was developed: the Tuguba Tribe of Komo and the Hiwa Tribe. Both parties to the dispute submitted 'traditional evidence', which largely involved evidence tracing genealogies to the respective apical ancestors who first arrived on the land and 'walked' (that is, the acts of hunting and foraging) the land or 'worked' (that is, making gardens, planting trees, establishing settlement) the land. Both parties traced competing genealogies spanning sixteen generations, and the evidence was so equally convincing that it prompted Justice Amet to marvel, thus: 'It is truly remarkable that generations and generations of ancestors could be so clearly remembered by name, going back to their believed origin and founding ancestors' (at p. 313). Regarding the evidence led by the Tuguba Tribe in particular, his Honour observed (at p. 313) thus:

The Tuguba Tribe, particularly, described mountain ranges, rivers, streams and lakes, valleys and caves by names, which it said proved that the Tuguba Tribe ancestors were the first men to set foot on the land. The Tuguba Tribe described names which are today identified with the Tuguba Tribe and clans.

Both disputing parties traditional evidence was so evenly convincing that his Honour refrained from finding in favour of one or the other and refused to award the ownership of the disputed land on the basis of evidence of genealogies and the other traditional evidence as presented before him. When his Honour took that step, he was moving away from judicially established precedents where earlier decisions such as the *State v Giddings* [1981] PNGLR 423 where Kearney DCJ decided that in a situation such as the one that Amet J found himself in, the tribunal of fact should approach the situation by 'testing competing traditional accounts by reference to recent and existing facts established by evidence, and seeing, in that light, which of the two competing accounts is more probable'(p. 430).

Instead Amet J took the following path, by first stating (pp. 314–15 of his judgement):

Whilst genealogy of ancestral origin might well have, in the past, been conclusive evidence of ownership, I am of the view that it is not the only evidence that is to be relied upon to confirm ownership at the present time. I believe that with fast development and considerable movement of tribes and clans from one region to another, factors which ought to be taken into account in determining ownership in the present context ought to be modified and more fluid than the traditional methods of determining ownership. In this context, therefore it would be of little valid significance to rely solely on genealogical oral history that traces man's origin thousands of years.... If that oral history traces the origin of a particular tribe or a people back thousands of years without taking into account any other factors since that time to the time of dispute, it would make determination of ownership of land totally meaningless if there had been numerous other intervening factors between the origin of that group of people to what the present circumstances are.

After stating these, rather well thought out reasons, Amet J continued:

In my view, as a matter of principle, the tribunal determining disputes of this nature ... ought to begin to develop a system of determining ownership of land which takes into account both traditional values and methods of determining ownership as well as the developmental aspirations and interests of a wider provincial and national community to arrive at principles which will be uniformly utilised and applied, consistent with the Constitution's directive to develop a consistent and coherent system of indigenous jurisprudence.

Eventually, his Honour then awarded ownership to those clans, including a clan from the opposing side, who were in possession of the disputed land or parts of the disputed land, when the land mapping officials of the State and the resource developers arrived to map out the land. 'Possession', or rather current occupation, was therefore considered to be the basis of ownership, not genealogy or such other traditional evidence. I have elsewhere criticised this decision, on the point that by ignoring genealogy as a basis of ownership of customary land, it sets a dangerous precedent because initial illegal occupation of customary land ('squatting') can then with the passage of time legitimise ownership. This of course will create more problems than we will ever be able to solve (Kalinoe 1993: 1). I do however agree with his Honour's reasoning that where there has been substantial movement and migration then possession can be a determining factor.

In reaching his decision, his Honour was largely influenced and consequently relied upon a study done earlier by Cooter (1989) where Cooter looked at some Local, District, and Provincial Land Court decisions, and arrived at the following principles. These have now been judicially adopted and were applied by Amet J in the Re Hides Gas Project Land Case. I quote some of these principles from pp. 318–19 of his Honour's judgement:

1. Adverse possession: A group that resides upon or occupies and improves land for sufficient period of time without active opposition from others thereby [establishes] a legitimate claim to ownership of it.
2. A group can be said to own the land by its ability to occupy and use the land and to stop others from doing so likewise, thereby showing that it exercises controlling interests over the land.
3. Maintenance of interest in land (or possessory acts): An interest in land is maintained by building houses and settling on it and by gardening, cutting and burning it off, hunting and collecting from it or forbidding others from occupying and using it.
4. No unqualified right of return: Once a group has abandoned its ancestral land by cutting all ties and associations with it, the group cannot return and claim it at a much later date without the agreement of those who prior to that date have assumed controlling rights to it.
5. Ownership presupposes control: Ownership implies the power, whether exercised or latent to occupy and use land and to stop others from doing so.

In handing down his decision, Amet J emphasised at p.319 of the judgement that: 'in the end result, the decision has been in favour of the clans who are in physical occupation of the land, supported principally by the principles I have relied on above, as supported by the evidence of "sufficient" period of time in occupation'. I hope that this goes some way to address the problem of 'squatting' and subsequently, legitimising ownership.

Justice Amet offered the following (albeit, *obiter)* caution and advice for future land courts and tribunals hearing dispute claims over customary land:

the decisions of conflict-resolving tribunals need to be based on principles that are fashioned on facts and circumstances which are relatively current and recent, and not too ancient. If Papua New Guinea society is to progress, it must be prepared to embrace some modern values as well as relying on some that are traditional(p.319).

The Bases of Ownership Claims to Customary Water Use Rights

In common law, water in its natural state is not capable of ownership given its mobile transcending nature. It is therefore not feasible to make ownership claims over water in rivers, lakes or streams. The common law also distinguishes between 'tidal navigable rivers' and 'non-tidal watercourses' and attributes specific legal consequences to them. The former (tidal navigable rivers) are effectively considered as State/Crown rivers and therefore not capable of private ownership, either of the watercourse itself or the fishery. The latter (non-tidal watercourses) are usually smaller watercourses, such as streams and lakes, are viewed more as 'the species of land' and therefore the water and the fishery are capable of ownership, particularly by the landowner. The principle of riparian rights however gives water use rights only to all riparian landowners' riparian land abutting either a tidal or non-tidal watercourse. The use of water associated with riparian rights is restricted to 'ordinary uses' associated with the riparian land tenure (for example, for domestic and stock watering purposes) and not for uses outside of that context.

In a study that I carried out from 1996 to 1997 looking at customary water use rights in some of the main inland water communities of Papua New Guinea (Kalinoe 1999), the people I encountered were of the view that although water as a substance in a river or stream cannot be owned, watercourses (rivers, streams, lakes etc.), whether tidal or non-tidal, are capable of ownership and are indeed owned by the landowning clans and such other lineages on whose land such watercourses flow or are located (as in the case of a lake). So by owning the watercourse, the people then indirectly claim ownership to the water and all other natural resources found in the body of the watercourse: fish, crocodiles, sand and gravel etc. With reference to ownership claims to tidal navigable rivers such as the Sepik, Ramu, Vailala, Purari and Fly, the people reasoned that although they, through the clans or lineage that they belong to, do not own (say) the entire Sepik River they do own those parts of the River which flow through their customary land. In other words, they own a part of the (Sepik) river, and all the resources therein, from the point at which the river flows through their land, and cease to own it when it leaves their part of the land; from then on the next (adjacent) clan on whose land the river flows then own that part of the river, and so on until the river empties into the sea. So, in the case of the Sepik River for example , there are obviously multiple owners to the river where their ownership of the particular part of the Sepik is defined by the land that they hold under customary land tenure. Although this concept of ownership is similar to the concept of riparian rights at common law, it differs however to the extent that ownership is not restricted to the extraction of water, but the claims include ownership of all the other natural resources and, furthermore, that the use of the water from the watercourse is not restricted to 'ordinary uses' as at common law, but all uses, including (say) a use outside of and unconnected with the riparian tenement.

The survey on customary water use rights referred to above (Kalinoe 1999) took in the upper Sepik River and Chambri Lakes (East Sepik Province); the lower Ramu River (Madang Province); lower Angabanga, Aroa, and Vanapa (Central Province); Vailala; Purari and Piie rivers (Gulf Province); Fly River and Lake Murray (Western Province); and Lake Kutubu and Lake Kopiago (Southern Highlands Province). In this survey, it was repeatedly and consistently stated that land ownership is the basis upon which ownership rights are claimed. Water use rights, as opposed to ownership rights, are not so much dependent on ownership of land, but on other factors like relationships with the landowning clans etc. So here there is a distinction between ownership rights and use rights.

Just as land use rights are held by a clan, rather than individual members of the clan, water use rights or even more so, watercourse ownership rights, are held by the clan or such other land owning lineage. However, in the case of a small watercourse (such as a small lake) it is possible that a certain family only may have ownership rights over that watercourse. With regard to ground water, it was agreed in all the villages covered in the survey that the clan that owns the land on which ground water is located has ownership rights over the ground water resource. But it is usually the case that after a well is sunk, when water is drawn every one in the village is allowed access. Those other people who come and draw water from the well fully acknowledge the ownership rights of the clan upon whose land the ground water is located and extracted.

As briefly introduced above, ownership rights over watercourses under the customs of the communities in the survey referred to above also include ownership of fishing rights. The people with ownership rights lay claim to the watercourses and the fish in them, usually to the exclusion of all outsiders or those who have no relationships with the clan or lineage that has ownership rights. Hence, those others (outsiders) are usually required to obtain permission from the elders of the watercourse owning clan before they can have access to their fishing grounds. The ownership rights claimed by the watercourse owning clans are generally accepted by other members of the community within the village, or communities within the same language group (as in the case of the Manambu, where there are three main villages, Avatip, Malu, and Yambon). The following example from the lower Ramu River, where an elder from another clan openly acknowledges the ownership rights of another clan, clearly demonstrates this. Within the communities or villages of Gwaia, Wunganam, Jeriken No1 and Jeriken No2, my informant told me that the Agur Clan was the dominant land owning clan in their communities and accordingly owned most of the watercourses around them, including parts of the Ramu River where it flows through their land. My informant there, Mr Hosea Blue, who was previously a village councillor, acknowledged the land and watercourse owning capacities of the Agur Clan, thus:

> Indeed, the part of the Ramu River we live in is owned by the Agur Clan. My clan, Kwai comes under them. Rivers and lakes are owned by the clan. For example, Agur Clan owns Iramkin lake and we use it from them (Kalinoe 1999: 238).

In instances where there appears to be over-fishing etc., resulting in very low levels of fish stocks or crocodile population, the watercourse (mainly lakes) owning clan, usually exercises ownership rights and places restrictions (on the type of fishing methods or the length and size of fishing nets) or outright bans prohibiting access to their lake or lakes. For example, in Gwaia village on the lower Ramu river, the landowning and hence lake owning clan, have placed a ban on three lakes, Kerf, Sinok and Iniora, from access and use mainly to allow for the crocodile stock in the villages to increase as previously there has been over-hunting of crocodiles resulting in the near depletion of the resource. The clan which 'owns' these lakes has placed bans under which no one, including the owners themselves, are allowed to go fishing or hunting crocodiles in these lakes for the following periods:

- Lake Kerf, for a period of eight years;
- Lake Sinok, for a period of four years; and
- Lake Iniora, for a period of five years

Generally all the other members of the village who used these lakes prior to the bans have accepted and since then respected the bans. In the event of any breach, compensation is payable to the lake owning clans (Kalinoe 1999: 239–40). The clan's authority to place these bans over these lakes, and then have other members of the community respect and observe such prohibitions, of course demonstrates, in no uncertain terms, the other people's recognition and acceptance of the clan's ownership rights.

As alluded to earlier, in customary water use rights there is a distinction between 'ownership' rights and 'use rights', where the latter does not confer property interest but only usufructuary rights. In the customary water use rights survey referred to above, all the communities covered in the survey accepted this distinction. Proprietary interest in the nature of ownership rights were mainly recognised to be accruing to or held on two primary bases: the ownership of riparian land; and the factor of first discovery of the particular watercourse, that is, ancestral discovery and use which are invariably clothed (masked?) with cosmology.

Other factors which do not give proprietary interests in customary water use rights, but mere usufructuary rights, are these: (a) the loss of a clansmen, relative or ancestor, in defending the territorial boundaries of the watercourse concerned from enemy or intertribal attack; (b) on the basis of long-term usage of a particular watercourse or a certain part of the watercourse which becomes recognised and is passed down from one generation to the next; and (c) through work done in cleaning and maintaining the watercourse concerned. The significance of the distinction between ownership rights as giving proprietary interest on the one hand, and mere use rights on the other, comes into prominence in three main situations: first, when dealing with an outside institution such as the national government or some resource developer; secondly, when contemplating and indeed engaging in the commercial exploitation of water resources; and thirdly, in times of scarcity. In the first instance, the national government or a resource developer has to consult and deal with the clan or such other lineage that has ownership rights and not those who have and exercise mere water use rights. This is where a distinction is drawn between 'true owners' and those 'others'. It is the clan or such other lineage that has ownership rights that can take a 'binding' decision on the use or access of a watercourse, not those 'others'. (Bear in mind that in a given watercourse, there are bound to be many 'owners' depending on the land that they own through their clan.) In the second instance, any activity that contemplates or indeed involves commercial exploitation of the water resources, such as commercial fishing or extraction of sand and gravel, is restricted to the 'owners' of the watercourses, not those 'others'. In the third situation, that is in times of scarcity, particularly during the dry seasons, it is those 'owners' who usually 'moot' or take initial steps to put in place appropriate restrictions or bans, and then through the village councillor, impose the restrictions or ban. In this situation, the 'owners' by using their ownership rights, act to 'save' the watercourse and the water resources therein. It is therefore 'ownership' that empowers these people to protect the fisheries and the watercourses they control. Necessarily then, these 'owners' also become the guardians of the watercourses they own, hence preventing the 'tragedy of the commons'.

Apart from the obvious focus on the resource access and use in customary water use rights, the survey that I undertook also overwhelmingly and consistently emphasised the use of certain parts of watercourses for traditional ceremonial and spiritual purposes. All the villages covered gave numerous examples of places or parts of watercourses which were of ceremonial, ritual or spiritual significance. Clearly, such places were revered. Through these relationships, people identified more affectionately with the watercourses or parts thereof as truly theirs, perhaps not in the strict sense of ownership, but more in the sense of 'belonging to' or 'togetherness'. Suddenly, the watercourse is then treated as one of them, as a subject rather than an object. This is particularly so when they paddle across parts of the river or lake and it is acknowledged that there is a 'river spirit', and that spirit is one of their totems to which they must give sacrifice if they want a successful fishing or crocodile hunting trip. I cite the following examples from the customary water use rights survey that I conducted in the upper Sepik River area:

> In Imombi, the area at which the May River meets the Sepik River is considered to be a sacred site and the locals believe that a mermaid lives there. So if the people want a good catch in fishing or crocodile hunting or even to successfully rescue a floating log, they offer sacrifices by throwing a big bunch of betelnuts into the area and ask for the spirit's help and good will; in Suagap, [when] people embark on the sago starch extraction process in the vicinity of a place of some spiritual significance, they have to call out to the spirits and ask permission to use the water to wash the sago fibre. In many instances, the consequences of not doing that have been that the sago starch did not settle and has been too watery (Kalinoe 1999: 214).

Conclusion

There is no doubt that the ownership of customary land is the primary basis upon which the indigenous people (customary landowners) in Papua New Guinea are making ownership claims to natural resources (those 'useful and beautiful things'). This covers practically all resources, including those which are not capable of legal possession, let alone 'ownership', at common law: in the case of water, resources include water in the watercourse; the watercourses themselves; and the fish in them. We have seen earlier in the common law case of *Young v Hichens* (1834) 6 Q.B. 606 that unless fish in watercourses are captured, and sufficiently and legally possessed, they cannot be owned. The situation in Papua New Guinea is different because statute law such as the *Water Resources Act* Chapter 205 (Revised Laws) and the *Fisheries Act 1994* recognise and preserve the customary landowners rights to access, legal possession and ownership of these resources. In fact most natural resources legislation in Papua New Guinea today recognises and preserves the customary landowners access, use and to some extent, ownership rights (see Kalinoe and Kuwimb 1996: 147).

Amet J's decision in *Re Hides Gas Land Project Case* [1993] PNGLR 309, as seen above, appears to now state the law on ownership in customary land tenure to be that in evenly contested customary landownership cases, the clan, tribe or such other lineage that is in physical possession (occupation) of the land will be awarded ownership. This decision further implies that a tribe, clan or such other group cannot, by tracing its genealogy to its related clan or tribe who are in physical possession (occupation), and through that relationship alone, stake out its ownership claim to the land. That relationship or 'tie' would not be sufficient for ownership. The claimants must be in physical occupation themselves to stake out their ownership to the land. This to me is the problematic part of the decision because this seems to suggest that genealogically traced and proved ancestral customary land (as evidenced by those related clans etc., in possession) can, under this decision, now be lost to another clan or lineage of a more recent occupation. The potential implication of this decision then is that a larger and more dominant clan or tribe can take adverse possession of a weaker or less populous clan or tribe and over passage of time, by the back door, acquire ownership!

In view of this, rather 'frightening' implication, I submitted earlier the following, and I now emphasise, that the Re Hides Gas Land Project decision must be approached with caution and:

> ...be interpreted in this manner:
> 1. That ancestral sites and genealogy are the first and primary factors in the determination of disputed customary land;
> 2. In the event that there is equally convincing evidence of genealogy, ancestral sites and clan names extending back a comparatively equal number of generations (as in the circumstances of this case), then those clans who physically occupy the land should generally be awarded ownership, in order to minimise hardship to those present occupants. In an extreme case, nevertheless, the decision could take into account considerations of equity, reasonableness and fairness, as warranted by the particular circumstances of the case (Kalinoe 1993: 11).

However, as the decision in the Re Hides Gas Land Project Case stands, the implications of this decision for other natural resources such as fisheries and all other water resources, particularly those obtaining under customary water use rights, appears to be that the clan or lineage who is in physical possession of customary riparian land will be accorded ownership rights (as opposed to use rights) in the event of a dispute. If that is the case, what will happen to those riparian landowning clansmen who do not live by the river banks, such as the Pinu villagers of the Aroa river (Gabadi area, Central Province) who only use the river occasionally for swimming and during the prawn season, but who still nevertheless claim customary water use rights? Do they lose their water use rights to those more recent settlers who were introduced by plantation labour requirements in the colonial days but now live on riparian land at the mouth of the river? Of course not. And that is exactly the problem with the *ratio decidendi* of the decision in Re Hides Gas Land Project case.

Notes

1. Now Chief Justice Amet. In the rest of this article I refer to his position at the time of this judgement. J refers to 'Justice', CJ to Chief Justice, P to President (Court of Appeal), and DCJ to Deputy Chief Justice.

6

Keeping the Network in View
Compensation Claims, Property, and Social Relations in Melanesia[1]

=========

Stuart Kirsch

What if culture were subject to copyright, patent and trademark law, as Michael Brown (1998) asked recently in a review essay on cultural property rights. He suggests that the application of these forms of ownership to culture could stop or slow the movement of ideas, reducing innovation in literature, art, music and other creative endeavours. Limiting access to cultural property seems incommensurate with liberal political values that emphasise the free and open exchange of information. While caution is clearly indicated with respect to the application of legal codes designed for commerce to cultural domains, Brown fails to take into account the various provisions for 'fair use' that accompany these laws. Furthermore, there is a growing body of knowledge that is already subject to private and corporate control; why should indigenous communities have fewer resources for controlling their intellectual property?

A more fundamental problem with Brown's approach to these issues is his assumption that Euro-American models of property and ownership are the necessary starting point for policy and/or legislation on cultural property rights. Alternatively, can Melanesian ways of investing in relationships and claiming rights to property be used as the basis for providing recognition and/or protection of indigenous knowledge and other forms of cultural property? The contributors to this volume attempt to provide answers to this question by presenting detailed ethnographic accounts of specific transactions. I focus on the social networks that are emphasised by compensation claims in Melanesia, but neglected by Euro-American models of ownership.

I examine three cases concerned with relations between the Lihir gold mine and local communities on the island of Lihir, east of the Papua New Guinea province of New Ireland.[2] The first two examples address compensation claims made against the mine for the loss of pigs. In the first case, the death of a number of pigs from Putput village was initially attributed to pollution from the mine. While scientific investigation eventually refuted these claims, compensation payments were made after the mine acknowledged a complex chain of events linking its actions to the death of the pigs. The second case is concerned with pigs killed along the road built by the mining company; it illustrates how both parties manipulate social networks to their own advantage. The final case examines new values for pigs in ritual exchange that appear 'irrational' or 'non-economic' unless one takes into account the longer social networks that are invoked by these transactions. Social networks are implicated in all of these examples. How do the mine and the local communities differ in their manipulation of social networks?

My argument is that the compensation claims examined here may be compared to patents or copyrights insofar as they involve statements about rights to things or ideas. However, there are substantial differences in the social relationships which they acknowledge. Whereas patents seek to shorten social networks in order to establish more exclusive claims to ownership (Strathern 1998b), compensation claims generally strive to keep the social network in view. In other words, Euro-American property claims place limits on ownership, while Melanesian compensation claims expand the possibilities of participation. The case regarding compensation claims for pigs killed along the road illustrates that there is some flexibility in the application of these strategies. In all of the examples considered here, however, the composition of the social network is central to claims about property, ownership and rights.

Although compensation claims made against mining companies may appear to be an unusual context for examining how Melanesians formulate claims to property, several advantages are apparent. The cases provide access to both Euro-American and Melanesian ways of viewing social networks in the same context, facilitating their comparison. Negotiations between employees of the mine (both expatriate and Melanesian) and local communities also provide commentary on their respective differences. Lihirians have had to adjust to the new world created around the mine and, in the majority of the cases examined here, they accomplish this by recognising wider social networks.

Case One: The Mysterious Demise of the Pigs at Putput

In late 1999, Samuel Venge* from Putput village in Lihir presented a compensation claim to Lihir Management Corporation (henceforth, the Lihir mine), which operates the gold mine at Lihir. Venge sought compensation for the death of two pigs that he was raising in the village, which includes property adjacent to the mine. In the heat of the afternoon, the pigs cooled themselves in Labarai creek, which runs behind the processing plant at the mine; Venge suggested that the animals also drank from the creek. Run-off from this facility apparently enters Labarai creek, leading Venge to conclude that pollution from the mine killed his pigs. He asked for compensation from the Lihir mine, holding it responsible for his loss.

The mine's manager for external relations, James Makon*, responded swiftly to Venge's claim. Makon, who is from New Ireland, previously directed community relations at the Ok Tedi mine, where communication between the mine and the communities located downstream from the project has long been dominated by mistrust. The Ok Tedi mine claimed that its environmental impacts were benign – a public relations poster from the 1980s asserted that *'Kampani lukautim wara, bus, na abus...'*, or 'The company protects the rivers, forests and wildlife' – while creating one of the largest environmental disasters in the Pacific. Makon's experiences at Ok Tedi encouraged him to expedite the response of the Lihir mine in order to allay suspicions that the company had something to hide. He spoke directly with Venge, negotiating the terms of the compensation, and authorised payment of K2,200, which was made in December.

Several days later, however, a representative from the Lihir Mining Area Landowners Association (henceforth, landowners association), speaking on behalf of twenty-one landowners from Putput, presented claims regarding the deaths of an additional twenty-two pigs to the Lihir mine. What caused the mysterious demise of the pigs at Putput? Did toxic chemicals from the processing plant poison the animals? Was the mine responsible for the decimation of the Putput pig herds? Should it compensate the owners, particularly given the precedent established by Makon with respect to Venge's pigs?

Early in the new year, a representative of the mine composed a memo describing his meeting with the villagers of Putput, who 'agreed that compensation is not the [sole] solution to their demands. We must identify [the] cause [of the pig deaths] and inform the community.'. In the interim, villagers from Putput requested that a fence be built around the plant site to keep their remaining pigs away from Labarai creek. As another mine employee related in a separate memo, 'If we can block [access to mine property] off...then we will solve the problem. Their pigs can die on their own side of the fence.'.

Shortly thereafter, the Lihir mine formally requested that the PNG National Agriculture Quarantine and Inspection Authority investigate the Putput pig fatalities. The regional Veterinary Officer arrived in Lihir two days later. He conducted ante- and post-mortem examinations of an affected pig and recorded his observations on local pig husbandry. His research suggested that the pig deaths were the result of 'the combination of over-population of free-ranging pigs, inadequate nutrition and severe contamination by internal parasites', rather than pollution from the mine, although there were elevated levels of lead and arsenic in the run-off from the processing plant (Thompson 2000: 11). He recommended that Labarai creek be diverted away from Putput village, suggesting that otherwise it would remain a 'cause of concern and possible basis for compensation claims.' (ibid: 12).

The mine faced a dilemma. While the regional Veterinary Officer absolved the mine of direct responsibility for the pig deaths, the residents of Putput rejected all attempts to limit the issue to a simplified or shortened causal hypothesis, i.e., whether or not the pigs died as a result of exposure to toxic chemicals contained in the run-off from the processing plant. Furthermore, they threatened to close down the mine if compensation was not forthcoming.

Eventually the mine decided to compensate the pig owners with outstanding claims. It also proposed to help remedy the conditions responsible for the porcine fatalities. What rationale did they present for their decision? A long series of events linked the mine to the death of the pigs. Construction of the mine forced the people of Putput village to relocate. Their new land lacked sufficient resources to adequately feed and support the number of pigs that they owned. This resulted in 'severe malnutrition and worms infestation due to improper feeding and unhygienic condition[s]...which the pigs encountered while in search of food', according to a memo written by a member of the mine's agricultural staff. Pressure from the landowners prompted the mine to acknowledge the complex chain of events through which it was connected to the pig deaths, leading it to accept partial liability for the losses incurred by the people of Putput.

In a draft of the settlement agreement between the mine and the pig owners, this was expressed as, 'LMC [Lihir Management Corporation] and the community of Putput...acknowledge that all parties must share the blame for the problem...' The agreement includes commitments from the mine to pay K17,640 in compensation for the lost pigs, institute a vaccination program as recommended by veterinary authorities, conduct an educational program regarding the care and feeding of pigs for the people of Putput village and undertake other actions in support of local pig husbandry as appropriate, including the monitoring of their health status until the current problems have abated.

While the mine initially regarded the events in relatively narrow terms, focused on scientific evidence that failed to reveal any connection between the mine and the death of the pigs of Putput, the villagers rejected this perspective. Negotiations between the two parties, which took place under the threat of mine closure, led the mine to acknowledge its implication in a wider chain of events that had unintended and unfortunate consequences for the people of Putput.

Networks and Ownership

It is instructive to examine this case in relation to comments made by Marilyn Strathern (1996, 1998b) in a pair of essays on networks and ownership, which were written in response to Bruno Latour's (1993) *We Have Never Been Modern*. Latour argues that a distinguishing feature of modern networks is their length, for example, the complex chains that move commodities throughout the world. In contrast, Latour argues that 'premodern' social networks are relatively short in length.[3] Strathern takes issue with Latour's claims, suggesting that he neglects differences in the way that societies construct and use networks, and examines how Euro-American ownership claims reduce the length of their networks.[4]

Returning to the example of the patent, when a firm seeks to license a scientific discovery, its claim to ownership is based on what it has contributed to the invention, and consequently it ignores contributions from pre-existing scientific networks (other scientists who have conducted research on the subject or invented the tools necessary for its discovery). A patent thus restricts ownership (and profit) to the final segment of the network, neglecting the other contributors. Strathern calls this 'cutting the network' and suggests that Euro-American models of ownership operate by limiting the number of claims to property. So whereas Latour describes the propensity of modern networks to grow large, there is an important caveat, that Euro-Americans tend to shorten these networks when they establish claims of ownership.

In contrast, Melanesian social networks typically include all of the persons who have contributed to another's success, each of whom may later lay claim to their share of whatever is produced. While Melanesian networks may not expand to the scale of their Euro-American counterparts, claims of ownership do not necessarily reduce their length. The threat of sorcery, for example, levied against persons who refuse to acknowledge their debts to others, can be seen to mitigate against the shortening of Melanesian networks.

These examples complicate Latour's assertions about the scale of networks. Both approaches to networks can be seen in the case of the pigs at Putput and in the mine's response to the community regarding its losses. On the one hand, the mine initially viewed the problem in terms of limiting its obligations to local communities. Compensation should not have been paid because pollution from the mine did not kill the pigs. On the other hand, pressure from Lihirians prompted the mine to acknowledge its implication in the lengthy chain of events that led to the problems at Putput. The mine's initial response was to shorten the network, while the Lihirians sought to keep the social network in view.

Science, Networks and Compensation Claims

One of the central issues in compensation claims made against mining companies is how science, like ownership, is associated with the shortening of networks. Scientific evidence is often used to reduce the complexity of a problem by framing it in relation to a 'natural world' that exists independently of social relations. Landowners affected by mining companies in Melanesia have challenged the exclusivity of scientific explanations, providing alternative perspectives which take social relations into account.

In several cases, the communities living downstream from mining projects in Papua New Guinea have claimed that the mines are responsible for problems that previously they would have attributed to sorcery. The Yonggom living downstream from Ok Tedi mine view it as a kind of corporate sorcerer which acts irrationally, behaves in an anti-social manner and endangers its neighbours (Kirsch 1997b). Their compensation claims against the mine cover a host of misfortunes – including a lost finger, a broken leg and a drowning after a canoe overturned – that implicate the mine in social relations downstream. Yonggom sorcery accusations critique the political economy of mining by invoking compensation claims against the mine which draw on the local moral economy.

Downstream from the Porgera mine, along the Strickland river, similar claims about sorcery have emerged (Haley 1996). Their assertions were initially limited to the deaths of pigs thought to have drunk polluted river water. The deaths were blamed on 'poison', which is a local euphemism for sorcery. This led them to view the mine's environmental impacts as a kind of sorcery. The analogy was later broadened to include human fatalities, so that a number of deaths initially attributed to sorcery via 'poison' were subsequently explained by pollution from the mine.

In both of these examples, the critical question is how to explain problems that local communities attribute to the mine. Euro-Americans look primarily to science to answer this question. Environmental issues are amenable to positivist, empirical inquiry. Either it can be demonstrated that the mine caused a particular problem (e.g., that the run-off from the processing plant at Lihir killed the pigs from Putput), or the mine is absolved of responsibility. But neither questions about compensation claims for pig deaths at Lihir or overturned canoes on the Ok Tedi can be fully answered by science alone. The tendency for Euro-Americans to view environmental issues independently of social relations follows the modernist emphasis on the separation of categories (e.g., nature/culture). Melanesians, however, are more apt to treat what Euro-Americans call the 'environment' as a hybrid, a combination of social relations and things in the world, in part a human creation, rather than an independent condition (e.g., the 'organic').

These examples suggest that science may be predicated on the same strategy that establishes ownership in 'modern' contexts, cutting the network. Latour emphasises the hybrid nature of these networks, their ability to combine persons, ideas and things (e.g., scientists, arguments about global warming and refrigerator coolant) into a single chain. Yet the narrow scope of science may prevent it from fully answering questions that are hybrid in composition. In contrast, Melanesian emphasis on social networks brings these other issues into view.

Case Two: Lihir Road Kill

When mining company vehicles kill domesticated pigs, which forage and move along the open road, Lihirians demand compensation. A system for addressing these claims is in place. A corporate representative is sent to negotiate, paying as much as K1,000 per pig, although the rate varies according to the original investment (some animals are now brought from Rabaul and New Ireland by sea, at considerable expense), market value (based on size and maturity at the time of death) and projected value at maturity (if not fully adult). These principles are not necessarily applied with consistency; social factors (the identity of the driver and the owners of the vehicle and the pig) and other details of the accident may influence compensation payments as well.[5]

One of the views expressed by some parties at the mine (both Melanesian and expatriate) is that Lihirians exploit these events to extract additional money from the mine, which is compelled to respond in order to maintain working relationships with the surrounding communities. Cited as justification for the corporate critique is the fact that Lihirians claim compensation from the company for *all* pigs killed by motor vehicles, even when the vehicles are not owned by the mine or driven by an employee. The Lihirians argue that because the mine built the road (although Lihirians requested its construction), it must provide compensation for every pig that is killed in a road accident.

Conversely, some Lihirians are critical of the mine's practice of paying compensation on behalf of its employees. The landowners association argues that the driver of the vehicle, rather than the mine, should compensate the owner of the pig. In practice, however, the mine, rather than the person driving, pays the cost of compensation. The landowners association argues that holding the drivers personally accountable will reduce the number of accidents along the road.

These examples demonstrate that Lihirians are not committed to a single strategy vis-à-vis social networks. On the one hand, they claim that the mine is responsible for all of the pigs that are killed by vehicles along the road, construing the network as broadly as possible (while also presumably avoiding negotiations with fellow Lihirians who are not employed by the mine). Yet on the other hand, when they assign responsibility for road accidents to individual drivers, they reduce the network to its shortest possible configuration. The mine, it might be added, employs both strategies as well: shortening the network to deny involvement in accidents which do not include either company vehicles or personnel, while lengthening the network to assume financial responsibility for all claims against its employees. These are strategic decisions; both miners and Melanesians may either shorten or lengthen social networks according to the circumstances and their objectives.

Case Three: The Exchange of Pigs

The pigs of Putput discussed in Case One were intended for ritual exchange involving inter-clan feasts held for major life-cycle events, of which mortuary rituals are the most significant. The value of the pigs distributed at these feasts is generally calculated in terms of shell strings known as *mis* in Tok Pisin. The production and distribution of both pigs and shells has increased significantly with the influx of cash from the mine. Rough-cut disks of shell are made in New Hanover, traded to Tabar and then acquired by Lihirians in exchange for pigs and tobacco, where they are polished for local exchange (Macintyre n.d.). Macintyre describes *mis* as 'genuine shell currency' comparable to Tolai *tambu*: it is divisible, used in everyday as well as ritual contexts and functions as a standard across both spheres of exchange.

Macintyre (n.d.) criticises essentialised views of Kula and other regional exchange networks, arguing that historically they did not represent separate spheres of exchange. Valuables were regularly diverted from exchange networks for other purposes. Contemporary patterns of exchange are simplified versions of past systems because the introduction of cash and manufactured goods forced other valuables out of circulation, often before the systems were described by ethnographers. Her argument is important with respect to Lihirian incorporation of cash and imported foodstuffs into their feasts; she emphasises the persistence of flexibility rather than the emergence of novel patterns of exchange. In particular, Macintyre takes issue with Foster (1996: 169), who cites with approval Strathern's observation that only with capitalism are different kinds of valuables fully commensurable (in other words, one of the novelties of capitalism is that it makes it possible to reckon the value of all goods in terms of other goods).[6]

Macintyre (n.d.) also describes how Lihirians increasingly travel to New Ireland to buy pigs at inflated values. On Lihir, producing pigs from cash is now an effective substitute for raising pigs oneself. Whereas being a big man was once synonymous with owning many pigs, today's big men compel mine workers to purchase animals on their behalf. As Macintyre (n.d.: 23) notes:

Lihirians will travel to Tanga or Tabar or Namatanai and pay up to K1000 (and numerous mis) for a pig that would cost less than half that on Lihir. The pig is usually large...but often indistinguishable from others acquired for less. At the feast this pig will be given and its very high cash value made known, so that the counter prestation will have to involve a pig that has been purchased for the same amount of money and mis. The economic 'irrationality' of this trend is not conceded.[7]

The expenses to procure pigs from other islands greatly inflate their value. Yet one's entire investment is measured in the exchange. It takes more than a pig of comparable value to match a pig in a subsequent exchange, it requires *a comparable investment*. Macintyre refers to this as irrational or non-economic.

In another sense, however, contained within the pigs that Lihirians exchange at their feasts is a series of transactions or a network of social relations. What people seek in return is not just an equivalent in economic terms; its qualitative value must also be matched. They measure relations with one another through pigs and what is being evaluated is the work or agency that is required to bring the pig to the feast, or more generally, to produce pigs in the context of the new world created around the mine. This takes the form of social networks that are, in effect, contained within the pigs themselves.

An analogy can be made between these exchanges and compensation claims made against the mine. When Lihirians seek compensation from the mine for one of their pigs, they also seek recompense for the network of social relations embodied by the animals. Compensation is expected to address their work and agency in producing these pigs as well as the lost potential for forming new relationships. Similarly in the Putput case, the manner in which Venge's pigs died implied a series of events (including their relocation, the inferior land on which they were forced to graze their pigs, etc.) that were also contained within these animals. In seeking compensation, Lihirians bring these (otherwise concealed) networks into view.

Conclusions

The debate between Strathern and Latour over networks provides a useful analytic framework through which to address compensation claims in Lihir. Latour overlooks relations of power between persons occupying different nodes along a network; Euro-American claims of ownership work (in part) by cutting networks short, whereas ownership claims in Melanesia usually bring social relations into view. It is important to note, however, that these are relative emphases rather than essential differences: as the disputes over compensation for pigs killed along the road in Lihir illustrate, either party may, on occasion, emphasise exclusivity over incorporation.

While Strathern reduces these networks to purely social terms (persons and their extended parts which take the form of objects), Latour emphasises their heterogeneity. That these networks incorporate a range of persons, things and ideas may account for the dissatisfaction of most Papua New Guineans with narrow scientific explanations of the environmental impacts of mining projects. The role of social networks is also apparent in exchange relations associated with mortuary feasts in Lihir. The value of the pigs given in their feasts represents the work and agency required to produce pigs through cash relations in the new world created around the mine. In all three cases considered here, it is constructive to think of pigs as embodying the social networks through which they were produced, as well as possibilities for future relationships.

The motive of this volume is not simply to bring indigenous ownership in line with Euro-American options by providing the same legal rights to Motuans over their tattoos that Disney has over its cartoons, or the same controls over certain varieties of sago to their cultivators that biotechnology firms have over the hybrid seed they produce. This is how arguments about cultural property rights are usually framed, as a response to the problem of Euro-Americans profiting (or profiteering) from the restricted ownership of knowledge and things in the form in which they are produced by Euro-Americans, while denying comparable rights to people in places like Papua New Guinea.

In contrast, the contributors to this volume emphasise the need to focus debates about cultural property rights on how Melanesians formulate claims to what they produce, use and transact. The compensation claims examined here suggest alternatives to Euro-American models of property with their truncated networks and explain why science may have difficulty in solving hybrid problems. They also suggest that any policies or legislation to recognise and/or protect indigenous knowledge or cultural property in Melanesia should keep the social network in view.

Notes

* Indicates pseudonyms.

1. This paper chapter has an unusual history. The Center for International Business Education (CIBE) at the University of Michigan provided funding for three weeks of research in Papua New Guinea on property and social relations from the miner's point of view. Circumstances beyond my control limited my stay on Lihir to a single day. However, the issues raised in my interviews proved to be of considerable interest and I have chosen to write about this material, supplemented by written records to which I was given access. Consequently, particular attention should be paid to the disclaimer that any errors of fact or interpretation are my responsibility alone. Some of the issues discussed here remain controversial and some of the readers of this paper have disagreed with portions of my argument. I would like to thank those persons who participated in interviews during my visit. I am grateful to Martha Macintyre for permission to cite her unpublished paper; both she and Michael Wood generously commented on this paper.

2. The Lihir group of islands (Niolam, Malie, Masahet and Mahur) is located off the east coast of New Ireland, between Tabar and Tanga.

3. See Harri Englund and James Leach (2000) for a critique of the meta-narratives embedded in the concept of modernity.

4. Tony Crook (2000) examines social networks and social responsibility in British debates about genetically modified agriculture.

5. Gender is also a factor in these cases. Macintyre (2000, personal communication) notes that compensation claims are always made by individual men, whereas in the past the pigs would either have been the property of families (with multiple ownership crossing gender lines) or individuals, with men and women having rights to equal numbers of pigs. The money obtained through compensation claims is individually controlled (and consumed), rather than circulated or re-invested. Women are usually denied access to these funds, even if they were responsible for the care and feeding of the animal. Social networks associated with compensation claims may contract in terms of gender when their losses are converted into cash.

6. Contrast Foster (1996: 167): 'An object of exchange functions as the singular measure of its own value and requires for reciprocation a replica of itself....In this regard, exchange objects, particularly shell discs, are better thought of as tokens instead of as currency. Put differently, no unitary, measurable quality, conceived as value-in-general, renders commensurable the diversity of value-forms given and received in exchange. Put less assertively, there is no necessity to presume such a conception of exchange-value in order to understand identical exchange. Equivalence is rendered axiomatic by the definition of exchange as a substitution of identical value-forms or replicas.'

7. Macintyre (2000, *personal communication*) also indicates that these payments may be seen as a means of redistributing cash from wage earners and the recipients of royalties to persons with less access to cash.

7

Combining Rationales from Bolivip
The Person and Property Rights
Legislation in Papua New Guinea

═══════════════

Tony Crook

Marriage involves each partner adapting their ways. Extended networks of relatives are drawn together by anticipating the kind of joint-person that may emerge from the combination. As such my discussion here is prompted by the long-arranged marriage between two rationales of ownership. I am interested here in the new joint-person to be created by Papua New Guinean ideas of ownership, and those of international intellectual property legislation (such as the World Trade Organisation sponsored Trade-related aspects of Intellectual Property Rights (TRIPS) agreement, and the UN sponsored Convention on Biological Diversity (CBD).[1] I use some examples of how Papua New Guineans combine rationales of ownership in order to look at this new legislative combination. Of course, Section 9 of the Papua New Guinea Constitution exclusively lays out the sources of law by combining statute law with the underlying law. The underlying law is itself already a combination of rationales: that is, of indigenous Papua New Guinean customs, and the common law of England as it stood at Independence in 1975 (Kalinoe n.d.).

As a British social anthropologist, I am drawn into the marriage through participating in a research project which involves collaborations with Papua New Guinean anthropological and legal scholars, as well as with a particular group of Papua New Guineans I have come to know over recent years. My contribution here is that of someone who himself carries a combination of rationales: those of Angkaiyakmin from Bolivip village in Western Province,[2] and those of Euro-American anthropology (Knauft 1999 provides a summary and guide to the history of interests that anthropologists have developed in Melanesia). I do not presume to speak exclusively for either side, but instead make the assumption that my own combination of these respective rationales enables a distinctive voice.

Let me begin then, by outlining my ways and how I intend to adapt them. Social anthropologists are concerned with the relationships people draw amongst themselves, the relations people draw between persons and things, and in the relationship between practices and the accounts that people give for their actions. Anthropologists work by considering how certain perceptions of persons and things involve particular relational connections. This method enables anthropologists to ask the same sorts of questions they might put to Papua New Guinean villagers as they would put to an international organisation, or ask of a piece of intended legislation. It asks: what social relations between persons, and between persons and things, are being combined here? Social anthropology then, 'makes use of the social relationships that are its subject matter', and operates by using 'the subject of study as the medium of that study.' (Weiner 1995: 11).

Opening this discussion with the picture of the new joint-person created by a marriage was quite deliberate. The subjects of this study are 'persons' created by combining 'rationales of ownership'. My method will be to use examples from Bolivip both to illustrate Angkaiyakmin rationales of ownership, and in order to anticipate the combinations involved in Papua New Guinea's intellectual property legislation. I wanted to make the complexities involved accessible, to make them into a more familiar example – the kind of metaphoric figures of speech or *tok piksa* that Angkaiyakmin use amongst themselves. My method, then, is borrowed from Bolivip where people often use one example (called *kukup*) to think about another example (see Crook 1999).

The proposed legislation anticipates a set of legal techniques to be employed in the business of combining with Papua New Guinea's resources and thereby increase trade. A feature of the Papua New Guinean response to these new legal measures has been the insistence that any knowledge or technique subsequently developed be returned and made available to Papua New Guineans for their own use, and a corresponding insistence that the measures amount to establishing an ongoing relationship. Going on the evidence so far, it seems that WTO and Papua New Guinea have different hopes for their legislative marriage: put bluntly, whereas WTO wants to create a legal object capable of carrying money, Papua New Guinea wants to create a legal person capable of carrying relations. Euro-Americans, such as those who have written the intellectual property legislation, tend to think of 'knowledge' as a kind of object, whereas I want to suggest that Angkaiyakmin think of it as a kind of person or subject (see Crook 1998).

Important knowledge in Bolivip (which concerns male initiations, land, clans, healing plants and garden magic) is understood by Angkaiyakmin to involve a combination of relations *which are similar to those involved in making a person.* For example, a young man will ask his father's side and mother's side to help him – the knowledge contributed from his father and mother's brother is then combined with his own understanding. We might even say of both the person who comes to hold such knowledge and the knowledge itself that each become a person made up of other people. In suggesting that an Angkaiyakmin person is made up of others each of whom has their own relation based on a particular rationale which might be used to make claims, the possibility is raised to talk of a person made up of different 'rationales of ownership' – for each supporter might have their own rationale.

This is why I talk about a kind of 'joint-person' which the combination of legislations will create (here I follow Riles's lead in regarding legal documents as 'persons'; see Riles 1998, and her edited volume on documents, n.d.). With this example in mind, we might then begin to think about the kind of person it might be, and the kinds of things we might expect this person to be able to do. I think it is fair to generalise and say that Papua New Guineans have their own developed sense of the relations which compose a person, of what particular capabilities a person has, of the kinds of claims that can and cannot be made of a person, and of what kinds of effects can be drawn out of a person and under which circumstances. These are intellectual resources close to hand with which to think about the new combination of legislations.

In the next section, I move on to Bolivip and take up the Angkaiyakmin assumption that there are always 'two sides' to everything, in order to illustrate the emphasis placed upon 'helping each other' (*dakoradakora*) and 'sorrowful feelings' (*kiinkiin*) in matters of ownership – two idioms drawn from a repertoire of practices that anthropologists would identify as 'social relationships'. To illustrate the force of claims to ownership made in these idioms, two case-studies are presented as examples of how rationales of ownership combine and compete with others. Having described the combinations of relations involved in making a person and in making knowledge in Bolivip, I will look at how these relations are 'un-combined' (see Mosko 1983), taken apart following a person's death when their relatives put forward claims to a share of the mortuary gift (called *kinim talin*). In such moments, the 'rationales of ownership' that made up a person in their life, are made explicit as people negotiate their different claims, and in doing so negotiate what kind of person the deceased had been – that is, they negotiate who else the person was, so to speak, and who amongst them is able to make which kinds of claims over what kinds of things. These two case studies teach that, in stressing the importance of the quality of social relationships rather than the qualities of the objects being claimed, Angkaiyakmin claims to ownership rarely operate through only one rationale (see Bercovitch 1994 for another Min example of rationales in combination). Their force is shaped by combining with other rationales, in much the way persons are a combination of others.

Bolivip Connections

Angkaiyakmin are a Faiwol speaking Min group of under a thousand people, originally from Telefomin and based in Bolivip village, now dispersed throughout six villages in Western Province, and in urban centres across the country, principally Tabubil and Kiunga townships which are connected with the Ok Tedi mine. For an anthropological overview of the Min area see Craig and Hyndman (1990), and Barth (1987).

In Bolivip, neither persons nor rationales of ownership ever stand alone: they are always connected with others. Examples of these relations are illustrated through images of forest trees and garden taro plants. Angkaiyakmin say that villagers are like the interlocking roots of the rainforest, depending on one another for support such as household exchanges of visiting, food and care. They say that standing alone a person would just get 'blown over'. Men are expected to spread themselves: people talk of the 'branches' developed by making gardens, and in addition men develop '*kinimbip*' – establishing exchange partners (called *lup,* seed) in other villages – and bring back the 'fruits'. Without this work, people say 'someone will just grow straight up, and drop their leaves underneath themselves'. The ancestor cult leader is likened to *walap*, one of the largest trees, and one upon which many others lean for support.

Angkaiyakmin marriages are formed with those beyond one's own *kinim miit* (lit. man base/origin; loosely – 'clan'). This principle of exogamy ensures that persons are necessarily composed of two sources of relations – in much the way I am suggesting that rationales of ownership combine with others. Angkaiyakmin trace their kin according to whether the relation passes through a male (*kinim kaiyak* – man side), or female (*wanang kaiyak* – woman side): all matrilateral kin are therefore *wanang kaiyak* (via mother), whereas patrilateral kin are either *wanang kaiyak* (via sister, or father's sister) or *kinim kaiyak* (via brother, father, father's brother). This gives a person's relations an asymmetrical cast: whereas 'man's side' belong to the same clan, 'woman's side' may comprise people from several clans, related by either sister, father's sister or mother. Relatives from two clans make up 'woman's side', whereas 'man's side' all belong to the same clan. Similarly, married women acquire membership of two clans to a greater extent than married men, being able to make claims on the basis of either father or husband (to their own clan and that of their husband).

In figuring kinship and relations, Angkaiyakmin draw on a number of idioms such that, even at such moments as brideprice prestations (*wanang karik*) or mortuary gifts (*kinim talim*) which make patrilineal 'clanship' explicit, one idiom extending a basis of relationality (here blood deemed to pass only from the father), is cut across and limited by other bases such as help (*dakoradakora*) given or other manifestations of 'sorrowful feelings' (*kiinkiin*), which are equally important considerations. Often the closeness of a relation is evidenced by the 'straightness of talk' (*weng turon*) used – respectfully indirect to affines and older people, direct with siblings or anyone else (regardless of an existing relation) with whom one has become close by 'looking after their skin' (*kal kiin moyamin*). For example, people often either 'turn their words' (*weng fakong*) or ask a sibling for assistance 'straight' but within earshot of affines, in order to leave people to realise for themselves what is being said, what is being asked of them (that is, for them to 'think with their heart', *aket fukanin*). By virtue of a combination of rationales, such as close residence, care or exchanges, people often find themselves contributing to a gift they will receive. Claims in one idiom are often supported or restricted by claims in another idiom, as if a person's relations are constantly refigured in step with the action of social life.

Angkaiyakmin trace the origin of their clans to Telefomin, several days walk away to the north-west. In common with other Min, Angkaiyakmin tell of the adventures of the 'Old Woman' – *Afek* – and her younger brother in recounting the sources of their customary 'paths' (*kukup miit; kukup leip*), the origins of the ground (*bakan miit*), and the origins of the 'clans'. This is public knowledge. In dispersing from Telefomin, clans came to Bolivip by various paths: some directly underground by means of now sealed-up paths (likened to the rhizome joining a mother taro plant and a new offshoot); some directly overground by specific mountain paths; others coming indirectly, either by emerging in another place before continuing overland, or coming to Bolivip after an interrupted overland journey. Consequently, Min groups regarding themselves as distinct, often share some clans in common nonetheless, and affording a double-view of relations with other communities underlaid by a history of conflict and continuing enmity. The spread of the ancestor cult throughout the region is also traced to Telefomin where the impressive *Telefolip* 'mother house' is connected to the *yolam* cult houses once the centre of every Min village. The efficacy of the cult practised in Bolivip is drawn in part from the *Telefolip* house regarded as a 'mother taro plant' (*iman aukun*) to Bolivip's 'taro child' (*iman man*): people say that were the mother to die all the children would die as a consequence. An image of a mother taro plant nourishing a host of child-shoots often emerges in Angkaiyakmin accounts of the region; both in terms of the region as a whole being connected to Telefomin (from the Strickland Gorge in the east, to Mt. Juliana across the western international border in Irian Jaya), and also in terms of the role of particular places. For example, both Oksapmin and Bultem (beneath the Mt. Fubilan mine site) – where, for Bolivip, the sun rises and sets, respectively – are seen as the source of taro, marsupials, types of stone-axes, particular wealth items, story forms and rituals. Equally, a village preparing to perform an initiation, or celebrate the opening of an airstrip, or hold a football tournament, will attract participants and supporters from other villages and groups.

Angkaiyakmin sometimes describe Bolivip as 'in the middle' – at some remove from the origins of certain effects in the region – and as further along from both Telefomin and Oksapmin which, by virtue of their positions, have the role of 'problem solvers'. In other moments, these connections and causalities are described through an image of a tree with its base, trunk and spreading branches: particular positions share capacities for movement with parts of a tree. For example, Bolivip is the 'base' (again *miit*) where people spend most time, and from where they go away to forest and garden houses for periods of up to a month. In a similar vein to places which periodically originate effects themselves, the Ok Tedi mine and Tabubil township have recently become crucial sources of relational connection (co-work and residence, marriage etc.), and growth effects (money from employment and royalty income) for all the Min communities in Papua New Guinea (see Jorgensen's overview, 1996). These contemporary tensions are evident in the question asked by young men in Bolivip: 'where is the root of Tamsimal?' Tamsimal was the renowned 'big man' at the time of Charles Karius and Ivan Champion's first contact administrative patrol visits to Bolivip in 1926–7, a man exemplifying Angkaiyakmin values and a source of pride. The question asks whether the 'root' is still the *yolam* in Bolivip, or whether it is in Tabubil, as some other young men calling Tamsimal's name there had suggested. People were left to ask themselves the other questions – 'who are the branches, who are the children?' Each of these connections within and beyond Bolivip constitute the paths along which relations travel as reasons for claiming ownership.

Case Study 1: Bringing Together Combinations in Knowledge

The first case study focuses upon 'important knowledge' called *awem* – names, stories and techniques which concern the origins of clans, land and fertility – which is followed as a path to success in gardening, hunting, exchange and marriage.

Although in certain situations men forcefully assert that *awem* and the processes it concerns would fail were it ever discovered by women, in other situations men will advise each other to tell *awem* to their wives. Similarly, in certain situations men will assert that *awem* should only be revealed during the male initiation rituals of the ancestor cult, while in other situations men take a ready interest in the revelations of *awem* that they might hear in the men's house or in some secluded place. As in other instances, revelations of *awem* risk attracting the attention of sorcerers – the potential benefits are balanced against the potential harm. How might we understand the apparent contradictions here – that men seem to be saying one thing and doing another? An answer becomes apparent in the stress placed on there being one path to learning *awem*: that is to 'look after the skin' of a renowned man or woman, to help and feel sorrow for them. This path is followed by men and women.[3] Let me explicate.

I introduced my discussion by suggesting that Angkaiyakmin regard knowledge as a kind of person, rather than a kind of object. We saw earlier how a person has relatives from two clans on their 'woman's side', and from one clan on their 'man's side'. A similar asymmetry appears in women's accounts of how children are conceived, that is, the combinations involved in a new person. Some women are well aware, it seems, of the men's belief that only a single substance is contributed by each partner. But these women assert that, in addition to these two substances, they must add a further substance themselves. Where the male party regards two things as sufficient, the female party knows that the mixture (and the subsequent new child), contains this exclusive further contribution. Both parties agree, however, that having sexual intercourse only once is not enough, and emphasize that repetitions are required. 'Repetition' is separately explained as crucial to the process of learning important knowledge and getting a story 'straight'. I want now to illustrate how persons from 'man's side' and 'woman's side' combine in a similar way when knowledge is being made, and therefore the sense in which I talk about knowledge itself as a person.

In addition to the path of cult initiations, *awem* concerning the clans and the ground are passed on and known within particular clans (although older people may know and are sometimes asked about the *awem* of other clans). *Awem* concerning these matters is held to be of equal or greater importance than that of Afek or the initiations. People say that if the *awem* concerning the creation of the clans and the ground were allowed to appear in an inappropriate form – made clear (*fitap*), rather than kept hidden (*ati*) – then people belonging to that clan would no longer grow but instead be reduced by poor skin, ill-health and death, and the crops grown in that ground would not grow, nor game be found. People say that putting such *awem* into an inappropriate form would render clans or the ground 'useless'. As in other contexts, revelations of *awem* risk the sanctions of sorcery (*biis*) if they appear inappropriate: for example, although speaking the names of forest spirit sites (*gung awem tem*) can provoke their wrath, clan-kin say that it is important that adults should know the names in case some are struck down and are unable to call the name in a formula to expel the ill effects. Equally, although an established path exists whereby younger people can properly learn *awem* from older people outside of the initiations, these relations risk attracting the attention of sorcerers.

Angkaiyakmin say that there is only one path to learning *awem*: one must 'look after the skin' of someone with renown: one must 'clean the sleep from their eyes', 'hear their talk', feel and show sorrow for them, fetch water and firewood, give them parts of marsupials and types of taro. Only then will they take equal care in making their advice and *awem* both 'clear' and 'straight'. This path is one that initiated men follow to learn the *awem* of their clan or ground, or *awem* not shown in the initiations or about initiations they have not yet been shown. Women can also follow this path, either to learn *awem* from their father or husband, or in order to learn about important women's knowledge from their female relatives: about techniques, for example, to shape the features of a newborn to make evident the care into which it has been born. Although both men and women are able to follow this path, people say that younger boys and girls would have their appearance and growth spoiled if they were exposed to *awem*. Only once a boy has joined the men's house, and a girl become married and a mother herself, are they deemed to be prepared for combinations with others: the form of their person has to be appropriate.

We have seen the positive and harmful effects that *awem* can have on skin; this sense is only reiterated by Angkaiyakmin terms – skin is *kal*, and 'knowledge' is *kál*; coming to know something can be likened to 'making skin' (*kál kerela*). In this sense, an exchange of 'skin' takes place: one party 'looks after the skin' of the other, who gives knowledge in return. As initiates grow, they are told to keep the knowledge, skills and advice they learn well hidden in their thighs. One old man became fond of telling me that his skin had gone onto mine, and my skin had gone onto his: I had looked after his skin, and he had given me his *awem*, and 'opened up the thigh' and given me his advice and strength (*sawa, lamlam*) from inside. It is as if we are now imagined to be encompassed by the same skin – what is ours to circulate, circulates within.

Men say that a father is the main source of *awem*, and a father is, of course, keen to make a son capable and strong. Indeed, during initiation beatings, men say that *kinim kaiyak* on the father's side will be the harshest as they try to impart more strength and bravery (*atur*), and that it is *wanang kaiyak* and affines who will look after an initiate (calling 'your mother is here', 'your sister is here'). Men also say that a mother's brother will also give *awem*, and that this will 'strengthen' that received from a father (the idiom used is *nanor nanor*, which is used to describe the solidifying of drying sago, and the congealing role of conception substances when mixed together). But 'making skin' is no straightforward task of passing an object of knowledge as a bounded unit from one person to another.

Old men describe how juniors (and the anthropologist) seem always to be talking of the same thing, always asking the same questions, whereas junior men say that old men do not think first before talking, they just 'break a new path through the forest' with their stories, jump from topic to topic, 'turn their words', 'only tell you half' (*mari* or *atuk*), and keep the important parts hidden. Indeed, often *awem* and *sawa* takes the form of sayings that merely juxtapose images and leave others to realise the connections for themselves and add what might be hidden inside: for example, juniors are told not to eat *kwiyam* (the ground cuscus) without being told why. When men experience stories jumping around, they describe the storyteller as *kutar kutar* – starting on one story and moving to another, beginning in the middle and then telling the start but leaving the rest out, only telling the end but not the base. The expression draws upon the habit of *kutal* (the black-tailed giant rat) to dart away and disappear, making it one of the hardest things to catch in the forest, which is why it is often only caught by dogs.

Senior men advise juniors that all the things they have been shown and told will eventually become 'one sentence'. Moreover, they say that, having listened to their father repeating things for them, they had put everything into 'one story' and found 'one path'. The experience for juniors and anyone being shown new knowledge is, however, very different from the experience of these old men whose advice is simply to look after one's father and to ask again and again until one has the stories straight. For old men, 'making skin' is the result of the joint work of a father and son. But the sons tell a different story.

Junior men describe their experience of getting *awem* straight as '*kim kurukuru taratara*' – 'bringing middle pieces together': besides adding their thoughts to what is being shown and told, they listen to what is being said and then decide what someone was trying to say, they decide what order something should have been told in, and wonder whether someone can possibly be telling them straight. In Tok Pisin and English, men express this as 'adding', and 'mixing' things together, but in Faiwol the repertoire is limited to '*damakdamak*' (*dam* – base, 'meat', body of something; *mak* – 'one'; the repetition brings them together) and '*taretare*' (*-tar*, to come), I began to understand that Angkaiyakmin take the participation and combination of people and things in the process of 'making skin' for granted. More than the additions just described, such men describe the crucial role of having *awem* from another source, usually from a mother's brother. They say that it is possible to hear a story again and decide which one is most complete and straighter, and learn about the bits left hidden or left out. Contributions from a mother's brother, then, are added to the joint work of a father and son, in much the way a mother's brother contributes to an initiation in the person of his sister when he calls 'mother is here!'

In each instance, an exclusive addition from a woman's side is added to joint work. It is as if 'conception' remains incomplete, allowing for further additions, as though certain capacities of father's side and mother's side are released to grow a person throughout life (much as parts of themselves are repeatedly given to an embryo), and withheld until the person's appearance suggests readiness. Angkaiyakmin knowledge, it seems, is necessarily the result of combined persons and takes the form of persons combined.

Case Study 2: Taking Apart Combinations in Death

The second case study focuses upon the different ways in which social relationships are figured, taking as an example the presentation of the mortuary gift (*kinim talin*) following a person's death. Several rationales come into combination and competition at such times.

One idiom of Angkaiyakmin kinship construes this gift as being from a person's 'man's side' kin to their 'woman's side' kin (that is, from *kinim kaiyak* to *wanang kaiyak*). However, running alongside or against this larger plan, are the particular social relations the dead person developed among those he or she lived with, exchanged with or chose to associate with. For example, if a person's children had not looked after them – but an 'unrelated' (*sak*) person had – then it might well be that this unrelated person, rather than the children, was taken around the forest, shown particular places and told about their origins. Any claims to the use of hunting or gardening ground would run against other people reminding the children that they neglected their parents and so have no places of their own now. At death, when a person's 'man's side' kin are perceived to have been careless, their 'woman's side' kin are likely to become angry and upset by the news of a death and come to visit the house of the deceased, both to cry and to express their anger through '*abip fukanin*' or '*abin tomtom*' – described as village thoughts or village beating. On these occasions, 'woman's side' kin may well complain to the 'man's side' kin in strong and direct terms about their lack of care. At such times, the person's 'man side' kin who live further away can join these visitors and act as if they were 'woman's side' kin. Here geographical distance cuts across social distance and allows people to swap sides for *abin tomtom*, and find themselves contributing to a gift for someone who lived close to them, or even receiving a gift that they should have contributed to.[4] Again, let me explicate.

With respect to any recognised cognate or affine, Angkaiyakmin are either *kinim kaiyak* or *wanang kaiyak*, depending on whether the relation passes through a male or female. The person upon whom these distinctions turn also places one reciprocally in the opposite group – in this sense, relations have two halves. For example, one is *kinim kaiyak* to one's mother (married women in this context share their husband's clan), and *wanang kaiyak* to her brother. This distinction informs many situations where preference is taken by *kinim kaiyak*. For example, a sister defers to her brothers – even younger ones – but especially the eldest, in the same way that *wanang kaiyak* defer to *kinim kaiyak* for permission to use ground for gardening. This reciprocal relationship dividing kin between 'man's side' and 'woman's side' is made clear by the mortuary gift (called *kinim talin* – 'man gift'). On these occasions the deceased man's side kin, organised by the eldest son in the family, assemble shells and other valuables (called *kisol*) to be given to the woman's side kin. This is a closely inspected symmetrical exchange: for example, the gift given after the death of one's mother will be reciprocated exactly – the number and variety of the valuables, the size of the pigs – after the death of her brother. By virtue of these kinship relations, the separation of relatives into one of the two sides should be most clear cut on these occasions: however, several other rationales and bases for relationships are also made visible.

For example, the kin whom people talk about as closest are called *muk atuk* (breast share); these are those whom people will always think about if there are pieces of pork or frogs, fish and marsupials to share. The term is flexibly used, and these distributed shares are often less than ideally shared. With the customary preference for wives to move to the hamlet and house of their husbands, there is often some distance between *muk atuk*: sisters and father's sisters may well live too far away to receive regular shares, although a morsel, however small it might be, deriving from an important gift will often be sent. Correspondingly, people living in close proximity with each other will sometimes call each other over to share a meal, perhaps of cooked pandanus juice squeezed over a platter of roasted taro, or share a cropped banana plant.

In these examples we see two manifestations of relational closeness: one which traces substance, the other that traces residence. They comprise two rationales. One rationale cuts across the other – father's sisters who live too far away are likely only to receive shares of the more important gifts.[5] These relationships are in this sense composed in an equivalent manner to a person: each relation is itself a combination of two sources – residence and substance. Closest man's side kin are effectively those with whom one shares both, but just as living further away can reduce the force of substantial ties, so it is that unrelated people who nonetheless look after each other's skin perform the caring actions that are distinctive of close kin. The more a woman's side person acts to look after the skin of someone, the more they behave as if they were man's side kin. The less a man's side relation visits someone due to living away, the less they behave a man's side kin are expected to. These rationales are convertible into each other here, and consequently people can appear on both sides of a mortuary gift or on the opposite side to that one might suppose. Neither man's side nor woman's side stand alone, nor do the various rationales composing a person or a relationship stand outside relations of combination.

This is clearly evident in the mortuary practice called *abip fukanin*, when the woman's side kin may assemble and come to demand the *kinim talin*. Many of the Angkaiyakmin villages are within a half or full day's walk, and two hamlets are within earshot of collected shouts from Bolivip. News of someone's death travels quickly: those within the hamlet will hear wails and crying from the deceased's house, those farther away will hear that something is up and soon find out the source. A network of short-wave radios connects the villages, community schools, mission stations and vegetable produce market in Tabubil. Word spreads very quickly. Of course, in many cases a person's death will have been anticipated and relatives may have travelled to the village already. Moreover, in most cases relatives on both sides will come together and remain in the house for some days before a burial is arranged: crying together, telling stories about the deceased and perhaps singing the sorrowful laments which women compose and sing throughout the following months when sorrow overtakes them. The songs tell of the character of the deceased, the ways for which they were known, the kindnesses they always showed, and of the places the person was associated with. For the night or two following death, the eldest son will spend the night alone with the corpse, hoping to learn from the spirit what or who was responsible for their death. If anything is learned this is likely only to be shared with siblings or someone else who has looked after the skin of this man. Such knowledge is treated like the important knowledge *awem*.

Once the burial and associated meal is complete, the *kinim kaiyak* kin will begin to contribute towards the mortuary gift and to make returns to those who have dug the grave and carried the corpse. The social relationships brought together, as it were, in the deceased are made visible by these contributions which in effect stand for or substitute for the relationships themselves. Those parts of other people – their care, help and support – which helped the deceased in life are revealed: as if they were removing the traces of deceased and returning them. Equally then, the impressions and effects that the deceased made on others are acknowledged in these moments: alongside the stories told beside the corpse and the laments sung over the coming weeks, these contributions also manifest the ways and activities of the deceased. In this sense the relational composition of the deceased – who else they were, so to speak – is made apparent. These other people might well include those who will later 'go around the back' and receive the gift, but make contributions nonetheless out of the sorrow they feel for someone who had looked after them.

Once the gift is assembled, the woman's side kin will be called to receive it – and in turn they will assemble to distribute the gift with a few closest kin taking charge and bearing in mind the care and assistance, and the kind of relationship a particular person had with the deceased. They will recall (and be reminded by others standing nearby in low voices) who amongst them has particular claims on various bases such as having supported the deceased with work or with contributions to an exchange, who amongst them heard the person's talk and who thought about them. This distribution makes the particular relational history of the deceased's life evident in a similar way that the assembly of the gift does: on both man's side and woman's side, the specific combinations of relational claims are exposed and taken apart.

In cases where the woman's side kin think that the person's death resulted from the man's side kin being disrespectful or lacking in care, then they will come as soon as the news is received. The rationale of distance shapes *abip fukanin* in several ways. As the woman's side approach the village they may have already armed themselves with sticks: anyone hearing or seeing them approach will sensibly hide in the forest or in other houses. Anyone in the path of the approaching group – and this includes everyone who by virtue of living closer is expected to have looked after the deceased – will be scared off, pushed aside or perhaps poked with a stick. As the group enters the village, they may hit houses, dogs, pigs and anyone foolish enough to be around may also receive a blow. Entering the hamlet of the deceased, emotions run higher still; in their weeping, people express anger that their relative is dead – when last seen the deceased was enjoying good health or telling that they had long known of this lack of care that has now finished them off. Coming close to the house, marita pandanus and bananas might be cut down, dogs clubbed or shot, the deceased's pigs will be found and killed, the house beaten, rocked or even attacked with axes: anyone here can expect a severe beating. Later these people may go to the deceased's taro gardens and pull out all the plants, harvest the corms for others to eat but destroy the planting stock itself such that no continuity is possible amongst those who have effectively severed their memories with the deceased by not caring for them sufficiently.

In the most charged instances, the group may enter the house to find the man's side kin sitting with their heads bowed in shame. There are stories of some people being attacked, having the racks of heavy firewood collapsed on top of them, and fire ashes thrown over them in return for their lack of care. These excesses of *abip fukanin* are reserved for those closest to the house where the deceased died – even if they bear no substantial relation – but who had some responsibility because they should have been the interlocking roots supporting the deceased. Of course, some amongst the group receiving the attacks may be regarded as having properly cared for the deceased, and will be spared the beatings, and have a portion of the taro garden left in place and marked for them specifically. Distinctions between kin are also made on the man's side, for example, if the deceased's closest 'man's side' clan kin had left the person in good health and gone off to stay in the gardens or forest for even one night before learning of the death, they might return and join the woman's side kin in their displays of anger.

These examples have illustrated the ways in which persons and their relations are regarded as combinations with others – while one source of constitutive relationality seems to have a forceful or unchallengeable rationale, such as 'substance', we have seen that it depends for its own capacities on its relations with others. The same might also be said of the partners to a marriage or of sources of legislation. If we regard them as a joint-person composed of relations from different sides, then these illustrations from Bolivip suggest a means to think through the sources combining to produce a new person. These Angkaiyakmin examples demonstrate that in terms of the composition of a person, *rationales are all equally effective* – substance amounts to a claim upon a person equivalent to claims based upon residential proximity. Whilst each may be a forceful rationale in its own right, when brought into a relationship of combination, they appear to be *only one amongst other ones*.

Conclusion

In the aftermath of failure to agree an agenda for the 'Millennium round' of free-trade talks at the WTO's 3rd Ministerial meeting in Seattle in December 1999, the Hon Michael Nali, Minister for Trade and Industry and leader of Papua New Guinea's delegation voiced concerns about 'transparency'. Papua New Guinea was not alone. In a joint statement, Papua New Guinea allied itself with other South Pacific Forum member states (Fiji, Vanuatu and the Solomon Islands). To make his point about direct participation in the Seattle decision making process, Nali drew an analogy with UN sponsored intergovernmental conventions which negotiate similar legal documents, and which he suggested were 'open ended' to all members. The basis of this openness is due to all UN members being equal partners – that is, all members are of equivalent status, each is one amongst other ones.

But the WTO is a very different organization in which the differences between the economies of members are an important factor in trade, and an important factor in membership participation. For example, the Seattle Ministerial Meeting 'established working groups open to all members on specific issues. In more restricted meetings, which proved necessary to move the negotiations along, we ensured that all interests were adequately represented.'[6] Closer inspection reveals that the 'more restricted meetings' were the paradoxically titled 'Committee of the Whole'. 'Whole' here refers not to the inclusion of all members, but to the business of the 3rd Ministerial meeting in total. The 'Committee of the Whole' involves the direct participation of only part of the WTO membership – those with the largest economies. While the whole membership participates in the working groups, only part of the membership participate in the 'Committee of the Whole'. Countries with delegates on the 'Committee' were free to send delegates to the working groups but this freedom was not reciprocal. What looked like 'adequate representation' to the WTO (perhaps thinking of the whole meeting), looked like a lack of 'transparency' to delegates from many developing countries including Papua New Guinea (thinking perhaps of the Committee of the Whole).

In terms of an economic rationale, Papua New Guinea's membership of the WTO is of a different status from, for example, the United States or the European Union. As the administrative body for the TRIPS agreement, the marriage between the WTO and Papua New Guinea is also somewhat unequal. Although signed up to the very same legislation, Papua New Guinea's participation in the terms of that agreement has been different from these larger economies. Moreover, Papua New Guinea's capacity to enforce or resist particular applications of TRIPS is similarly unequal by virtue of economic differences.

But a different view appears when we employ the intellectual resources of the examples from Bolivip. Now, just as 'substance' appears at certain times to be the overriding rationale against which other rationales look insubstantial in Bolivip, so in terms of the rationales composing the WTO, 'economics' and the Euro-American concerns of the TRIPS legislation appears to be the overriding rationale. Limited to these terms, Papua New Guinea appears to be at an unchangeable disadvantage – yet it has its own resources, its own examples to draw upon. This paper has outlined some of these resources through examples drawn from Bolivip, and aimed to provide a means by which to approach the new legislation as if it were itself a person – and thereby be in a position to use Melanesian notions of the relations such a person might be able to carry and create.

Several points in the way Angkaiyakmin regard knowledge as necessarily the result of combined persons and to take the form of persons combined, suggest themselves as useful examples:

1. Michael Nali's dissatisfaction over 'transparency' was expressed by joining a group of others – this reminded me of the assembled woman's side kin in Bolivip protesting to the man's side. Whereas members of the UN hold a formal and equivalent status, the WTO membership is based on a different rationale: *rather than one side there are two*. We might think of

the Committee of the Whole as equivalent to the man's side clan kin in Bolivip: only some people belong there. But notice how the activities of the man's side were closely shaped by the woman's side.

2. The case-studies from Bolivip showed that rationales were equivalent bases or paths for relationships: important knowledge supposedly reserved for initiated men can flow to both uninitiated men and women along the relational pathway of helping each other, and looking after skin; relations based on 'residence' were shown to be equivalent to those based on 'substance' when it came to making contributions to the mortuary gift and joining in with *abip fukanin*. However forceful the international legislation may look, it is only one component among other components: in this sense it has an equivalence with the Papua New Guinean policies designed to monitor its implementation.

3. The Angkaiyakmin accounts of how a new person is conceived put me in mind of the ongoing discussions in Papua New Guinea regarding the *Custom Recognition Act (Chapter 19, Revised Laws)*.[7] Recall that Angkaiyakmin women suggest that in addition to the joint contributions of partners, one of the partners makes an additional and exclusive contribution, without which the new person would remain incomplete. With the room for developing the 'underlying law' through the process set out under the *Custom Recognition Act*, Papua New Guinea has the opportunity of making the rationales of ownership of its rural population one component amongst other ones – in other words, to make the rationales of people like the Angkaiyakmin into components of *equivalent status* to the WTO TRIPS component – *as one amongst other ones*. Regarding the combination of rationales in this way poses the position of Papua New Guinean rationales of ownership as a real issue.

My anthropologist's view of these legal matters can only look naive to lawyers – as if seeing only one half of things: only the trees and not the forest. But for their own part, anthropologists can add the kinds of detailed ethnographic examples employed here to make another half to things appear: that is, to show what view of the forest one gets when one looks at them as if they were a group of trees. The examples used in this paper are provided in the knowledge that they are only one, limited and anthropological, half to things. I have aimed to demonstrate that Papua New Guinea has resources to hand in order to think through a view of the TRIPS agreement as if it were a person combining different rationales, and therefore capable of carrying relations. Deciding the capacities and composition of this new joint-person rests with Papua New Guineans. Marriage involves each partner adapting their ways.

Notes

1. Papua New Guinea became a signatory to the World Trade Organisation and the Trade Related aspects of Intellectual Property in June 1998, under the terms of the agreement Papua New Guinea is obligated to enact domestic legislation by December 2000. Under the United Nation's Environment Programme's Convention on Biological Diversity, which Papua New Guinea ratified in 1992, domestic legislation is required.
2. This chapter results from research in Bolivip village, Western province during 1994–96, 1997 and 1999, and was written under the auspices of the British Academy as Post-doctoral Research Fellow in the Dept. of Social Anthropology, University of Edinburgh. Research in Western Province was facilitated by the Dept. of Western Province and the National Research Institute, and supported by an ESRC studentship, and the RAI/Sutasoma Award. I am grateful to Angkaiyakmin who assisted this research and to the various bodies whose support afforded me the opportunity to study in Western Province.
3. Barth (1975) provides an extended study of ritual and knowledge from a different perspective.
4. Battaglia (1990) and De Coppet (1995) provide examples of how mortuary responses produce new relations, drawn from elsewhere in Melanesia.
5. See Strathern (1996) for discussion of this process of cutting across.
6. Mike Moore, WTO Director-General. WTO Press/160, footnote omitted.
7. See, for example, contributions to the *Melanesian Law Journal*, Volume 21, 1993, and Aleck and Rannells (1995).

8

Global and Local Contexts

Marilyn Strathern

In 1997 two striking disputes concerning property relations and human rights preoccupied the Papua New Guinea press. They would appear to have little in common. The 'Hagahai blood saga', widely reported in the international press and debated on the internet, pointed to global interests in Papua New Guinea's resources created (in this instance) by medical technology. The second case,[1] on the other hand, concerned a revival of local practices in exchange and marriage arrangements, and the relevance of traditional values in a modern world. However, much is to be gained from taking the two together. Each throws light on questions about ownership and how people construct rationales for their claims. And together they raise questions about the contexts we create for understanding – whether as contestants, adjudicators or observers. What I emphasise here are contexts created out of what we choose to make of general or universal as opposed to particular or local relevance. The one case attracted international attention, while the other appeared of local (national) concern; but does this mean that the former is of more *general* interest than the latter?

The cases differ in an important respect. Information about the first comes from numerous published reports and papers, anthropological and otherwise; reference to the Hagahai may be longer or shorter, but frequently they are cited in the context of discussion explicitly aimed at issues which arise from other concerns as well. The story 'belongs', we could say, to an international world of commentators and journalists to which Papua New Guineans also contribute.[2] The second case has been the subject of one quite detailed anthropological analysis; I have also relied on the full report of the judicial findings and some local press cuttings.[3] However, there is a sense in which the account given here 'belongs' particularly to Dr John Muke of the University of Papua New Guinea; not only was he involved in this dispute, but his seminar paper, subtitled 'Kinship on Trial', delivered in Cambridge in 1996, has been an inspiration for my remarks.[4]

Case One: Hagahai on the International Stage

A Media Event

A tiny population living in the Schrader ranges on the northern borders of the Highlands, within the Madang Province, the people known as Hagahai were said to have been discovered in 1983/4.[5] In 1997, the 'discovery' was re-discovered by the media, national and international. Indeed for some Papua New Guinean television presenters, Hagahai stood for a pristine world now lost, for people suddenly catapulted into the late twentieth century.

They had the eye of the media because they found themselves caught up in a phenomenon that signals both modernity and globalisation: the development of biotechnology. With the biotechnology came the possibility of realising assets. Patent rights to any future commercial advantage that might accrue from products derived ultimately from blood cells 'collected' from Hagahai people had been filed in the United States. Dispute was over the kinds of interests Hagahai might have in the matter. Different rationales of ownership were brought forward, resting on and reinforcing perceived divisions between the developed and developing worlds, between Modernity and Tradition. The emergent discourses of intellectual property play further on these divisions (where developing countries have ancient customs and natural resources, developed countries show ever novel inventiveness and industrial know-how).[6] So the rationales for ownership appear for some peoples to lie embedded in cultural traditions invented long ago, while other peoples point to the rights they acquire from their progressive and innovative technology. What should we make of these two contexts as they applied to this case? Let us look at how they were established.

Illustrated by a photograph of two men in traditional dress, a caption to a short article in the *British Medical Journal* (2 December 1995) reads: 'Tribesmen are selling their genes.' In 1983/4, Euro-Americans themselves hardly had the language for imagining genes as market commodities, and here are *tribesmen* selling genes! The pace of innovation and the romance of first contact go together. 'A little more than a decade ago, these forgotten people were living in isolation...Today the 315 surviving Hagahai find themselves at the cutting edge of human endeavour, the centre of an international imbroglio thanks to the rapid advances in biotechnology.' (*The Australian*, 14 November 1995). An American news network put about a similar story some months later:

> The story of the Hagahai tribesman, of how the United States of America patented the blood cells of one of Earth's most primitive citizens, could only be a tale from the bioengineered '90s, a time when the prehistoric can still come face to face with the futuristic, and the technology of tomorrow often outwits the society of today. (20 April 1996, love@Essential.org)[7]

It was out of such conjunctions that 'the Hagahai' were accorded a historic role in the development of public awareness about intellectual property. A Port Moresby journalist reporting on Papua New Guinea joining the World Intellectual Property Organisation wrote: 'For the first time since Independence, PNG will make this remarkable stride, seen as a bold move to seriously address the issue of intellectual property rights (IPR).' Indeed he claimed that intellectual property has become *the* issue in Papua New Guinea. 'The move to accede to the WIPO convention would not have been fuelled without the recent controversial Hagahai...saga.' He then adds that without a reliable IPR regime PNG remains a haven for 'biological prospectors', 'biopirates' and 'bounty hunters'.

> The Hagahai saga also reveals the truth about the general vulnerability of our rich biodiversity, our traditional knowledge, folklore, designs etc. to exploitation by leading commercially-weaned foreign scientists and their cohorts, particularly the pharmaceutical companies. (Sinclair Solomon, *The National* [PNG], 31 January 1997)

In the background lay a complex story. Briefly, an American medical anthropologist, Carol Jenkins, concerned about the health of the Hagahai people had been taking blood samples from them. One pooled sample showed up a virus which in other populations leads to severe leukaemia but in this population appeared to have no such effect; the discovery of Hagahai immunity had global implications for understanding leukaemia related diseases. Antibodies (T-cells) were subsequently separated from the blood of one (unnamed) man infected with the virus, and a cell line (cells reproduced from an original) was cultured in an American laboratory.[8] US law at that point required that the inventors of the procedure for isolating the 'Papua New Guinea Human T-Lymphotropic Virus' should lodge a patent application.[9] The medical anthropologist later claimed that she had discussed the matter with Hagahai people, and, insofar as was possible, had their consent. She had signed her name to the patent with the intention that they would receive her share of royalties should commercial advantage ever result.[10] Having her name there was, in her defence, the only responsible way in which she could have protected the possible future interests of these people. Papua New Guinean authorities did not know about the signing; when the incident became public, there was a furore which led initially to her exoneration but eventually to her leaving the country.

The issues surrounding the patent stimulated calls for open discussion. The Director of the Institute of Medical Research to which Jenkins was attached, spelled this out. 'Since the virus grows only in human T lymphocytes [T-cells]…it had to be deposited in a human cell line.'; but while it was not human genetic information as such that was being patented, he observed, the patenting of any biological information raises complex isues. 'There is a need for an international review of the patenting of biological information, so that the ethical, legal and economic issues can be addressed and a common code of practice agreed upon.' (*Uni Tavur*, 23 February 1995). This he wrote in a student newspaper in response to attacks on the whole issue of patenting human material (in particular, an article called 'The challenge of the Hagahai blood saga'). It was the fact that patents confer ownership of exclusive rights to exploitation (for a limited period) that was the focus of concern.

The language used to decry the action was reminiscent of similar language used in Europe when the European Parliament was debating a directive on the Legal Protection of Biotechnological Inventions in 1995. But this is not a coincidental juxtaposition of mine, a matter of echoes or allusions: it is the very same language. These concerns are globalised in common rhetorics of ownership.

An officer with the PNG Department of Foreign Affairs and former newspaper reporter, Dominic Sengi, who repeatedly drew public attention to the Hagahai case in the national press, commented on the fact that the Commission of the European Union were (in his words) 'seeking a directive that would allow the patenting of all human, animal and plant tissue.' What he found interesting was the range of opinion Europeans voiced over the propriety of patenting biotechnological inventions, the divisions which had emerged, and the outright protest. At that point (April 1996), the European Parliament's view was that genes and cell lines removed from the human body did not constitute an invention and as such were not patentable. Sengi's words could have been found in any European newspaper:

I ponder privately to ask some basic questions. Who owns your body: you, society, a scientific outfit or a business? Biological sciences have for some time been raising serious social, legal, ethical, political and economic questions which are being addressed at a far slower rate than the advances in the scientific field itself. (*The Independent* [PNG], April 5 1996)

However, he prefaces it by saying: 'Bearing in mind the cultural attachment and significance Papua New Guineans associate with blood...'. I shall return to this.

Not many months later, the British newspaper, *The Guardian* (27 November 1997) had further cause to refer to the Hagahai.[11] The headline banner was 'Signing up to a patent on life'. The context was a renewed (and this time successful) attempt on the part of the European Union to formulate a Biotechnology Directive; the article was about the wide-ranging implications of the EU's desire to harmonise the laws of different member states in order not to lose competitiveness in these developments. European protestors, the *Guardian* said, take an 'emotive view about the risks of allowing life to be patented' and they

> talk about the Hagahai, people in the remote highlands of Papua New Guinea, who had their first contact with the outside world in 1984. Blood samples were collected after they had been exposed to viruses,[12] and later the National Institute of Health in the US was granted a patent on a Hagahai's man's cell line (which was later overturned).

Although they are being cited as citizens of one country over whose body products another country has acquired jurisdiction,[13] an interesting enough conundrum in itself, the Hagahai seemingly stand for the innocent human being in us all on whose very 'life' biotechnology purchases an option. Hagahai are being cited, then, not just for their own interests in the matter but for the universal and canonical status they seem to have acquired in media debate.

Beyond the journalists is a network of NGOs. Indeed it was well publicised, by themselves and others, that it was a Canadian NGO, Rural Advancement Foundation International (RAFI), which in 1995 first 'discovered' the Hagahai patent episode and felt they were fulfilling a responsibility to the world by disseminating the information.[14] There is in any case nothing unusual about syndicated features or about newspapers appropriating one another's news. Like the ubiquitous commodity, however, we could say that the resultant language tends to universalise certain Euro-American assumptions about property and ownership. Or, if we agree that there are some highly general concerns about 'ownership' here, we could say that they are being presented through one very local and particular (Euro-American) way of conceptualising them. At any rate, a rather specific context for 'global' interest is created.

It is also a language of protest. Reporters borrow from one another phrases such as 'patenting life'.[15] If the EU directive evoked a whole register of concerns (cf. Strathern 1999, chapter 8), the Hagahai saga produced ones almost identical in genre. Headlines included 'Making money out of DNA' (*The Australian*, 4 November 1995); 'Scientists attacked for "patenting" Pacific tribe' (*Science*, 11 November 1995); 'Indigenous person...claimed in US Government patent' (RAFI, 27 November 1995), and both the phrases 'patent a person' (*New York Times* 27 November 1995) and, from the internet, 'patenting a man'. But there is an even more interesting verbal consensus. Quite aside from the leaps from cell line to genes to life to person to man,[16] it summons a concrete symbol: blood. What fuels this global context, then, are images presumed to have universal appeal.

When Sengi says we should be bearing in mind the cultural attachment and significance Papua New Guineans associate with blood, isn't he echoing what could be ascribed to almost any culture in the world? Isn't the same true of Europe? On attachment and significance:

> There is a bond that links all men and women in the world so closely and intimately that every difference of colour, religious belief and cultural heritage is insignificant beside it.... [T]he life stream of blood that runs in the veins of every member of the human race proves that the family of man is a reality. (Titmuss, writing from the UK, 1997 [1970]: 61)

Although this dates from 1970, it resonates with Euro-American sentiments accompanying the accusations that 'life' or 'nature' is being 'patented' ('blood tie' is often used for 'genetic tie'). It carries metaphorical power. And it has to be the value Euro-Americans give blood as a potent cultural symbol that in turn gives power to this piece of rhetoric from the American news network already quoted [see n.7]: 'He's out there somewhere in the wild gorges of the Yuat River, hunting pig, harvesting yam, a young tribesman whose heart belongs to the jungle – but whose *blood* belongs to the US Government' (my emphasis).

A general attachment, or the fact that blood has symbolic associations, belongs to a global context, one which Papua New Guineans share with many others. Yet Sengi is right to suggest that blood has a specific and particular value for many Papua New Guineans. The particular value lies in how blood and other body substances become a rationale for payments between persons. They also become a rationale for an ownership of a kind. Here we can imagine a local (Papua New Guinean) context.

Before I turn to that, we might reflect on the way contrasts and divisions build up different contexts for people's understanding of their circumstances. The (local) world of the Hagahai and the (global) world which both produces biotechnology and supports the media that reports upon itself could not seem more different. Papua New Guinean, American and British reporters alike dwell on the gap between the state of the Hagahai and the technology that has brought them into prominence. On the other side is a story of a remote people with natural properties (the possible medical uses which could be made of resistance to the virus) which only the technology of the developed world can realise – realise both the significance of and the assets therefrom. Thus does a common international language divide the developed from the developing. It is the universal plight of the underdeveloped, ripe for exploitation, which gives the Hagahai global status as visible victims of the developed world.

Selling and Other Transactions

The caption to the *BMJ* illustration referred to tribesmen selling their genes. We have seen that 'tribesman' is part of the global discourse for drawing attention to the pace of (Euro-American) innovation; we have also seen that it was not 'genes' that were the subject of the patent.[17] But what about 'selling'?

If one were to take a lead from the 1992 Convention on Biological Diversity,[18] one might almost say that the problem was that the Hagahai themselves were *not* in a position to sell anything of the kind; it was scientists elsewhere who turned the cells into an invention they might conceivably sell. The whole tenor of the Convention as it affects the Third World is to encourage people to appreciate the significance of their natural resources. It wishes to facilitate technological developments in bio-resources (and directs contracting parties to put IPR legislation in place where appropriate), to encourage technology transfer to the benefit of those without, and makes special reference to the different responsibilities of developed and developing countries. For example: Article 15 (Access to Genetic Resources) specifies that each contracting party is to take legislative and other steps with the aim of sharing in a fair and equitable way the results of research and development, and the benefits arising from the utilisation of genetic resources (para 7). Needing to strike a new balance between developed and developing countries leads to suppositions about what forms of remuneration would be possible for other categories, such as use of indigenous knowledge (art. 8). Thus governments are advised to adopt policies that 'will protect indigenous intellectual and cultural property and the right to preserve customary and administrative systems and practices' (Agenda 21, ch. 26, my emphasis). Together these create a field of expectations about *what* might be realisable as an asset, a context for giving entities of all kinds new kinds of values.

One issue running through the charges of exploitation in the Hagahai case was that these people were somehow losing assets – that someone somewhere else would be profiting from what was theirs. The medical anthropologist was reported as justifying her action in exactly those terms.

Following a comment to the effect that if the Third World is to be protected from the unfair distribution of profits, legal mechanisms for protection must be implemented,

> Jenkins says she saw it [the patent] quite simply as an opportunity to get some money back for the community in return for their co-operation with the scientific fraternity. 'It is traditional in Papua New Guinea society if you take or injure bone, blood or flesh of any sort, that it be paid for...that's standard PNG law.' (*The Australian,* 4 November 1995)

Now it might sound as though 'pay' refers to buying and selling. But, as Radin (1996) has argued, we do not have to read the commodity into every monetary transaction. True, the Hagahai might at some future date get a return on an asset realised in the classical commodity sense – it becomes an asset where there is a market for it (the market gives it a value). However, a crucial issue here was that people should receive recompense for something that had been taken from them. The situation is much more like one of *compensation*. Compensation is paid for a harm or loss, understood as a value acknowledging but necessarily not commensurate with the value of the loss. Papua New Guineans are familiar with compensation being paid by mining operators or timber extractors for all kinds of loss of local resources, and claimed in addition to royalty agreements (cf. Toft 1997). Recompense for loss can thus work as a monetary, without being a market, transaction. The commercial benefits which Jenkins thought might have been brought to the Hagahai would not have to imply that body tissue was for sale, only that it had originally 'belonged' to them. Belonging does not necessarily imply ownership, let alone property ownership; but had the benefits eventuated then they and no-one else would own the rights to, and enjoy property in, the royalties and compensation payments.

However, from new practices of remuneration new claims to ownership arise. And if body substance can be realised as an asset over which rights are owned, then it could start looking as though it is the substance itself which is 'owned'. What was once inalienable (there was neither the technology to remove it nor the remuneration to give it a price) now starts looking like an alienable thing (*res*) over which an ownership claim can be made. These are just the rationales of ownership which Euro-Americans might see. They run together both the notion of what is inalienable, so that its loss is an injury which requires recompense, *and* the idea that if something can be taken away and find a market then it is rendered alienable and should be paid a fair price.

Sengi drew a parallel with the 1990 John Moore case in the United States. Moore had tried to assert property over a cell line developed from his spleen, and was not only defeated because the invention of the cell line did not belong to him but was upbraided by one judge for improper commercial motives in relation to his own body.[19] Sengi invokes its prior inalienability: 'In feeling a sense of "essence rape" the patient [Moore] said, "What the doctors had done was to claim that my humanity, my genetic essence, was their invention and their property. They viewed me as a mine from which to extract biological material. I was harvested."' (*The National*, 5 April 1997).[20] His person had been assaulted. However, commentators considering the property rights which others had actually gained for themselves through the cell line (in this case rights to a very lucrative product) might well have wanted to argue, on Moore's behalf, that he was the original proprietor of bodily material from which he should obtain profit if profit were to be obtained (see e.g. Frow 1997: 156–7; Rabinow 1996, chap. 7).

The Hagahai scandal, in RAFI eyes, was that the Hagahai man had 'ceased to own his genetic material'(Press release, 4 October 1995) – never a legal possibility of course. Yet whether monetary return would really have righted this other wrong is not debated. Instead the two ideas are allowed to run in parallel. For the one thing that the NGO and other protestors never said of the Hagahai was that it would have been wrong for them to receive the royalties. Rather, there was a case for compensation in addition to royalties. Thus RAFI complained that 'although one of the "inventors"…apparently signed an agreement giving a percentage of any royalties to the Hagahai, the patent makes no concrete provision for the Hagahai to receive *compensation* for becoming the property of the US Government' (Press release, 4 October 1995, my emphasis). Here we have just the kind of context created by the novel reasons for remuneration to which I have referred. The US Government (NIH) had made alienable what should not have been, but since they had done so anyway then it was their responsibility to see that resources flowed back to those from whom the cell line had been taken. These reasons are promulgated as though they were universal norms.

Whether one is talking of a commercial transaction or of compensation, new practices of remuneration create new social divisions between persons. These lie in what they might obtain in return for what they have transferred, had taken from them or otherwise lost. The entity in question may have been derived from body substances which cannot be sold by the person from whom they came but which applications of biotechnology can turn into a profit-yielding asset. I return to the point that the 'global' context created by media interest, which presented the Hagahai plight as a general case to touch all of us, also introduces certain particular Euro-American ideas about ownership with respect to body substance.

It is no surprise that whole parts of the world are divided off from one another in terms of what they can own and realise as assets. The Hagahai's supposed problem was that they could not work the technology for themselves. But nor were they just locals. They stood for, became a global icon of, peoples everywhere exploited by the new technologies.[21] What is taken to be 'local' and what is taken to be 'global' is not mapped on to relations between the developed and developing worlds in any simple way. But I have been drawing the contradictions and convergences here from a wide field. The case that follows deals with a single set of claims which turned very precisely on the 'local' or 'global' import of events. These dimensions provided the contexts for a set of legal proceedings and directly influenced their outcome. The case itself extends our understanding of transactions over 'blood', indeed of the specific notion that payments for blood can indicate ownership of 'life' or 'a person'.

Case Two: Defending Custom in the New Guinea Highlands

Kompensesen

Where RAFI had appealed to principles of compensation as a universal expectation, Jenkins asserted that compensation practices were entrenched in local tradition. The two would thus appear to reinforce each other, especially as it seems that in recent years compensation practices are being taken up in places in Papua New Guinea where they were not known before (Filer 1997). But, about the same time, a challenge was thrown down by another group of NGO activists, the Individual and Community Rights Advocacy Forum (ICRAF) based in Port Moresby. Whether or not they would have defended the idea of Hagahai getting recompense, here they aborted preparations for compensation well on the way to completion. The universal norms to which they appealed were not those of compensatory justice but of human rights in terms of individual liberty.

Two tribes[22] were transacting with each other over the taking of life. Literally, someone had died; metaphorically, the loss of the person was like the loss of body substance where the clan is understood to be the body which has suffered. The claim was for a man once inalienably tied to his kinsmen and clansmen, but now by an act of homicide cut off from them. Moreover, although there were monetary elements to the transaction, at its centre was a non-monetary component. Yet it was this component that was objected to most strenuously. So why, as it was reported in the national media (*Post Courier*, 11 February 1997; *National*, 12 February 1997), did the judge order that the two 'tribes' were to refrain from enforcing their custom? The central issue was the means of compensation.

Payment for a man's death had been agreed between clans from Tangilka and Konumbuka tribes, in the Minj part of the Wahgi valley, Western

Highlands Province. A Tangilka man, Koidam Willingal, had been killed by police; he was said to have been the bodyguard of a wanted man, a fact disputed by his kin. The final settlement comprised 24 pigs, K20,000 money, and a woman (Miriam, the dead man's daughter), who was to be sent to the aggrieved clan in marriage.[23] The aggrieved in this case was not the clan of the dead man – on the contrary, it is they who were being asked for compensation; the demands came from his mother's clan in Konumbuka. The rationale was that the deceased's patriclan had not protected their 'child' (their nephew, sister's child). This was at once a particular accusation (Tangilka had been responsible by causing the police to venture deep into their territory), and a general one (they had failed in their care of him where the maternal kin had not). Each side had had responsibilities for him in their own way, and was thus liable towards the other. To restore the situation, the aggrieved Konombuka demanded that a 'return' for Willingal's mother be sent them in marriage. The two sides came to an agreement and, as she 'was the only marriageable woman available' (Gewertz and Errington 1999: 125), Miriam emerged as the obvious person; she was to be part of the 'head payment' (death compensation). It was her position in all of this that drew the attention of ICRAF, a body which exists to educate people in understanding their human rights and legal entitlements as enshrined in the laws of Papua New Guinea. The pigs had been handed over; the rest of the settlement would have gone ahead but for their intervention.

The grounds on which ICRAF assumed responsibility for taking the matter to court, as summed up by Gewertz and Errington (1999: 125), were that, 'regardless of local custom, trading in women could not be allowed because it was violation of fundamental human rights.' They pursued the principle by seeking a series of orders from the National Court in Mt. Hagen to enforce Miriam's constitutional rights (see Sean Dorney's commentary in *The Independent* [PNG], 14 February 1997). The universal context and the national context here converge. Papua New Guinea's constitution embraces fundamental human rights, and Justice Salamo Injia, adjudicating, found that this particular compensation payment for the life of a human being was inconsistent with several provisions of the National Constitution. It was a clear matter of national law taking precedence over 'traditional customs'. Here one of his concerns was with the exercise of agency: how voluntarily had Miriam agreed to the settlement? He concluded that she was coerced into giving her consent, finding for ICRAF on the several issues they had raised.

Minj tradition was taken as an important context for people's actions. Indeed the judge paid considerable attention to unravelling the intricate background to the compensation settlement, helped by an extensive and detailed affidavit provided by John Muke,[24] and warned about quick judgements from outside bodies – including the 'modern courts'. But, reciprocally, tradition itself is thereby put outside the purview of universal human rights. It supplements the understanding of people's local motivations; it does not itself appear as a source of universal principles. (This allows internal distinctions to be made: not all parts of tradition need be supported at any one time.) While Justice Injia could see no objection to payment as such, and said that customary compensation practices involving 'money, pigs and other valuable personal items' ('things') were no problem, when the payment takes 'the form of single young women' ('persons') that is another matter (PNGLR 1997: 130, cf. *National*, 12 February 1997). Customary law is subject not only to the constitution but to the proviso that, cast in terms of a universal, it does not offend 'general principles of humanity'. This he invoked when he said: 'Living men or women should not be allowed to be dealt with as part of compensation payment under any circumstances.' (PNGLR 1997: 151).

Tradition is also put outside the purview of modernity (not his terms). Active measures had to be taken. 'No matter how painful it may be to the small ethnic society concerned, such bad customs must give way to the dictates of our modern national laws.' (PNGLR 1997: 153, quoted in *The Independent* [PNG], 14 February 1997). Equating modernity with a universalistic or global vision of human rights, then, would imply that customary law and tradition do not enshrine universal values – only particular, local and traditional ones. There is no evidence that Justice Injia intended this reading – indeed he carefully spelled out the continuing benefits of tradition; the need to prioritise (modern national laws over local customs) only arose because of an apparent conflict of values, and by implication there need be no conflict. Nonetheless the impression which the press reports leave is that what is traditional and local is inevitably overridden by the modern and the global. In fact there would seem to be some very *general* issues here, although one has to understand the 'traditional' and 'local' contexts in order to elucidate them. I suggest that if we look in detail at the rationales of ownership, we may find that the actions of the Minj tribes have something of universal interest to say.

Obligation

In order to understand who owns what and who owes what to whom, it is necessary to bring together into one context death payments owed to maternal kin ('head pay'), sometimes involving traffic in persons, and the debts created by marriage arrangements between kin. Muke (PNGLR 1997: 132; and see O'Hanlon and Frankland 1986) thus classifies head pay as a life-cycle payment, not to be confused with direct compensation by the killers to a victim's kin for homicide. In these terms, Miriam was not part of a compensation payment at all. However the term 'compensation' does capture some of the obligatory reciprocity behind life-cycle payments, and if I continue to use the term it is with this broader connotation in mind.

One of the rationales for compensation for loss of persons rests in the ties that bind them to others, notably their kin. Women are regarded as moving along the same channels along which wealth flows. They create 'blood ties' between groups, since the children they bear become consanguineal connections for the descendants. It is appropriate that payments follow these blood ties insofar as women's work and fertility bring benefit to their husband's rather than natal – father's, brother's – clan.[25] So one clan will indemnify another first for a bride and then for the children the woman bears. 'Blood' is salient among the reasons why payments for the child (the child's body) are due.

In an 'unnatural death', as this was called, when blood is shed, ties with the deceased's relatives are severed in an untimely way. A death payment is thus more than redress for a lost life; it involves a whole set of suppositions about the way persons are involved in one another's lives. When his maternal clan claimed that they had watched over Willingal's life and health, given it divine blessing and enabled him and thus his clan to prosper, they were also pointing to the subsequent severance of the flow of nurture whose road was created by that first marriage of his mother into Tangilka. The point of that, in turn, is that the flow of wealth they anticipated receiving in recognition for their nurture and benign influence was also severed by the death. Moreover, other marriages had followed, and the balance had been much to Tangilka's benefit. In finding recompense for this now blocked path, if they also provided a new bride the paternal kin would be helping to redress an old imbalance.

In the eyes of his maternal kin, Willingal was part of themselves (his mother's clan) also embodied as the member of another (his father's clan). The clan body engages in flows of wealth through claims made on what kin own of it and what, through the 'bodies' (offspring) they produce, they owe to one another. No-one can go around selling bits of body – any more than an industrial worker can sell his energies outside an industry that wants them – but everyone is enmeshed in a set of relationships predicated on exchanges of wealth between persons in recognition of the bodily energy and activities persons bestow on one another. The bestowal of women in marriage was, in men's eyes, part and parcel of these flows. The body does not have to be turned into a 'thing' in order to elicit wealth; it remains a part of the 'person'.[26] And it is not realisable as a market item; it is *realisable for specific others*. So a person's very substance may be thought of as belonging to another. As a consequence, who pays and who receives delimits two different sets of ownership claims.[27] We may talk of two rationales. Whatever age the offspring, the mother's clan 'own' the child because they are due wealth for it; the father's clan 'own' the child because they pay wealth for it.

The metaphors which Wahgi (Minj) people use of body payments draw these various aspects together into one context. When a clan sends out its women in marriage, it contributes to the prosperity of other clans; through these offshoots – a sister's child is called a 'transplant', as Muke points out – maternal kin expand their own spheres of influence. Injury to these progeny is injury to something they own, because what they own is what they are in turn owed. In local idiom, the deceased's 'bones' or 'head' (male wealth as appropriately given by the patriclan) should be sent back by the paternal clan to the maternal clan which had in its lifetime overseen his or her welfare (Muke, PNGLR 1997: 132). When kin seek, as they sometimes did, an alternative to or augmentation of other forms of payment by requesting that a granddaughter of the woman be returned, they talked of returning the 'head' or 'skull' in a 'netbag'. This referred to the strength or wealth (bones) of a woman's progeny in and within the form of another woman (the netbag), as Muke (PNGLR 1997: 132) and O'Hanlon and Frankland (1986) describe.[28] The metaphorical context in which these idioms have currency could not be more local.

It was while he was still composing the evidence he would bring to court that John Muke pinpointed the crux of the matter for himself, as a clansman and an observer, in his seminar paper: kinship was on trial (see n. 4). Not him or his clan mates on trial, or the deceased's tribe, or the Wahgi people, or Papua New Guinea custom and tradition, but what was on trial was a nexus of relationships which he typified in *universal* terms, 'kinship'. What was on trial, then, was a set of suppositions – the nature of relationships as a matter of people's conduct and obligations towards one another, the way we 'own' one another – of a kind which is found everywhere. In effect, he was creating a global context in which to ask his questions. What does one do about obligations embedded in the relationships one has with others? This is a highly general and universally relevant question, one which could be asked of anyone. The Minj case offered a particular version of this general problematic: what does one do about the fact that one clan is in perpetual spiritual debt to another for the welfare of its progeny? Let us look at the details, at the local rationales of ownership, from which this (general and universal) context emerges.

The case concerning Miriam and her divided (maternal against paternal) kinsfolk is all about the nature of obligations and how people meet the debts they perceive, although men and women are differently positioned here. These obligations derive from people's general connections to one another (respect owed, say) as well as from their own history of interactions (what happened last time). So there were many reasons why it was Miriam who was selected for the compensation. There were the responsibilities her kin had in relation to her.[29] But there were in addition many strands of relationships, of personal and clan histories, past events and old debts being brought together in what would be the 'one' transaction that would, it was hoped, answer them all. But that one transaction was in turn to be composed of diverse items of wealth, collected by several individuals from a range of others, under the circumstances where each contributor to the compensation payment would find himself faced with competing demands on his resources. 'Choices' had to be made (focusing on one out of multiple ways of acting). If acting requires choosing between alternatives, these are basically choices between relations – and invariably invoke prior relations. Here one arrives at an understanding of agency rather different from those enshrined in the human rights determinations of personal liberty. *Agency is evinced in the ability of persons to (actively) orient themselves to or align themselves with particular relationships.* This is not the same as free choice.

Miriam implied that she initially agreed to the compensation settlement out of the concern and responsibility she felt for her younger sisters and other clanswomen who might be asked if she refused (Gewertz and Errington 1999: 125–6). In her affidavit, she said that she was willing to be part of her father's 'head pay', but not willing to marry immediately or to marry just anyone.[30] Whatever one might think about her predicament, whatever pressure she was under, and whatever the imbalance in men's and women's freedoms in the matter, we are left with the fact of relationship: how to take into account the obligations which they entail, one person's dependence on another.

Evidence for these relationships lies in the body itself. Health and well-being are regarded as the outcome of actions on the part of specific other persons through their connections with the person in question. In the past, it was not any, generic, woman who would satisfy the maternal kin's demands. A particular relationship was singled out: she should be someone linked through the appropriate ties of substance. In this case the criterion would be met by someone standing in the relation of granddaughter to the specific woman earlier sent in marriage (the 'first blood', Muke [PNGLR 1997: 133]) and whose specific descendants had (as in this case) been injured.[31] Hence the importance of each side owning 'a granddaughter', embodied in Miriam, whom one could give and the other receive.

The sympathetic judge took all this on board in his response. Nonetheless he was obliged (so to speak) to object to the degree of obligation (PNGLR 1997: 149). Justice Injia found that obliging a woman to be part of a 'head payment' was an infringement of her constitutional rights, for example to play an equal role with men in the development of the country. Her right to equality of treatment was violated because the custom only targeted eligible women and not men.[32] Moreover, while an open request placed an obligation on all of a clan's girls, the closer the relationship then the greater the pressure. The question of 'pressure' is interesting. Locating the issue of obligation as an obligation owed to a *group,* the tribal groups and clans, envisages a community whose interests were clearly against those of the individual. If the human rights concern focuses on the way in which groups bring pressure to bear on individuals, then obligations start looking like cultural constraints, and cultural constraints somehow belong to the domain of tradition and custom. Tradition becomes oppressive. Yet when Miriam herself talked she had in mind specific individual kin, 'living men and women', of whom she was thinking. She was after all an agent in this herself. It was in 'thinking on' (Pidgin idiom) or being oriented towards her kin that her agency was manifest. During an interview with the Port Moresby *Post Courier* (20 February 1997), she said she was fearful about the way her clanspeople would interpret 'the law' (the judgement which had been given a few days earlier). She was reported as wanting her people to really understand the court's decision: her worry was that '[h]er people think the court has given her "freedom" from a traditional obligation and this could take away her tribal support.'

We are dealing with claims which bear in on the actors as immediate reasons for their actions, based on the fact of their relationships with one another. Yet to acknowledge claims as 'obligations' in the context of kinship looks to modern eyes as perpetuating dependency, control and coercion. Human rights discourse – grounded in equality between individuals – sweeps all this away. Is it also to sweep away kinship as such? That was Muke's arresting and searching question.

The General and the Particular

Judge Injia's thoughtful rehearsal of the evidence before him allows one to think again about what is taken as of particular, local interest and what speaks to general and universal concerns. I have picked out obligations as a dimension to *all* human relationships – not so different from the concept of dependency recently revived by MacIntyre (1999). Obligations as they are filtered through kinship offer a condensed version of this universal, simply because kinship is the sphere above all others where relations present themselves as inevitably prior in the life of individual persons.

It is arguable that such considerations are not or cannot possibly be of interest to the law. 'Obligations' of this kind belong perhaps to the same moral order as the claims, made in the Hagahai case, that recognition was due those who were the origin or source of a profit-bearing asset. In the quasi-legal language of intellectual property, perhaps we could say the Hagahai were owed a moral (rather than economic) right.[33] Yet those who took on the responsibility of speaking on behalf of the Hagahai were also demanding recompense in material form. In Minj, the origin or source of the prosperity which one clan enjoyed was traceable to an original marriage from another, and the head pay settlement was being used as the explicit occasion on which to acknowledge several debts.[34] Maternal kin were already owners of a moral right (to acknowledgement); they wanted it to be realised in payment. And where rights are thus expressed through transactions, the giving and receiving of items entail economic expectations which people are certainly ready to go to law about.

When such obligations are owed, by one person to another, they take on the character of a debt, quite as much as of a right, and any discussion of ownership in Papua New Guinea should probably at some juncture turn to what is entailed in 'owning' a debt. But I have raised the question of obligation with another purpose in mind. This was to think again about what is taken as of particular, and what of general, interest. *I wish to question the failure to recognise universal conditions in local circumstances.*

The genius of Papua New Guinea customary law as part of the underlying law is that, when legal solutions to disputes are sought, it allows variable reference to local moralities. This means that they can be taken on board piecemeal if necessary (as in the distinction made between parts of Minj custom). But precisely because of this particularity, it is the Constitution and the universal human rights principles it enshrines which appear to be of general import, as against purely local practices which in themselves do not appear to be of general import at all. In order to cut across these associations, I have drawn deliberate and rather gross attention to the effects that contexts have upon our reasoning. I dwelt on the contexts created by appeals to Tradition and Modernity, or to the Local and Global, and I have showed them in caricature (some of the newspaper reporting on the Hagahai) as well as in more sober light.

Much of the rhetorical justification for tradition is cast in terms of allowing people (the 'right') to practice their customs as they always have done; conversely critiques of conservatism perceive cultures as clinging onto practices which modern sensitivities may find repugnant. Yet an anthropologist might observe of Miriam's case that there was more to the actions of the two tribes than 'tradition' and 'custom'. Interaction between the maternal and paternal clans was carried by the persons caught up in the case. And from their viewpoint, they were involved in specific sets of relations to one another. While it may be consciously in accord with customary values that they follow this or that path, the motivation to act *also* comes from the claims which bind them to specific others. The specificity is misleading if we read it in too narrow a sense. For what is universal is of course *the specificity of relationships everywhere.*[35] So while these may be local examples, they are examples of a thoroughly trans-local social fact.

People cannot avoid relationships. This is true in a double sense: (a) conceptually, relationships have a momentum and character of their own, that is, each must take the form of a 'relation' and thus embody a particular image of itself; (b) in its acting out, each relationship involves other parties, at a minimum in sustaining the relationship. Some people are of course less free than others in this regard, and I would not want to overlook the differences between the pressures put on men and on women in particular circumstances. Nonetheless, to put words into Miriam's mouth that one might want to put into *anyone's* mouth, perhaps she would like to be free to fulfil her obligations. Or we could draw words from more than two millennia ago, and Sophocles' portrayal of Antigone who is caught between her responsibilities towards a sibling and the obedience she owes the state. In defiance of the King's orders, she attempts to bury her slain brother as kinship obligation dictates.[36]

The evident dangers of this line of reasoning – oppression in the guise of duty – are precisely those against which human rights provisions are very properly put into place. Yet these two very different cases have shown people of all kinds taking responsibility for others, to better or worse effect, and sometimes weaving those responsibilities into their rationales for ownership, sometimes not.

Notes

1. It became known as the 'compo girl' case, but Miriam (see below) is quoted as saying that she found it embarrassing to be referred to as the 'compo girl' (e.g. *Post Courier*, 20 February 1997).

2. For example, Cunningham 1998; Frow 1997: 153-4; Kirsch 1997a; Mangi 1998; Posey and Dutfield 1996: 26–7; Pottage 1998; Salisbury 1988 and several other articles in *Research in Melanesia*, most recently 1994, 1996. Cunningham and Pottage both cite articles by Jenkins, and papers in *Science, Nature* and *Social Science and Medicine*. *Cultural Survival Quarterly* (vol. 20: 1996) devoted a special issue to it.

   Many thanks to Jo Mangi for his observations on his visit to the Schraders. And also to Stuart Kirsch for materials on the ensuing RAFI controversy (see below). My brief time in Papua New Guinea in 1997 was made possible by the National Research Institute of Papua New Guinea, Conservation Melanesia and the University of Cambridge.

3. The case was heard by the National Court of Justice, 21 June 1996 and 10 February 1997, PNG Law Reports 1997, 123–54. I am very grateful to Lawrence Kalinoe for this extract from the Reports. An extensive summary and analysis is provided by Gewertz and Errington (1999, chapter 6), who mention it was reported in the *New York Times*. Ethnographic material on the Wahgi area is to be found, for example, in the works of John Muke, Michael O'Hanlon and Marie Reay (not cited here).

4. Based on my recollections of the paper given to the Cambridge Social Anthropology Department (Muke n.d.). I also draw on these materials in 'Losing (out on) Intellectual Resources' for the colloquium, Fabrications: the Technique of Ownership, sponsored by the *Modern Law Review*, London School of Economics, 1999.

5. The status of their 'discovery' is thoroughly controversial, as the long-standing debate in *Research in Melanesia* attests. See Kirsch 1997a on the advantage some may see in creating themselves as newly discovered 'lost' peoples.

6. Patent regimes specifically protect the knowledge bound up in inventions proved to be both new and with industrial/commercial application. Categories of Euro-American intellectual property

also embrace copyright, based on uniqueness of form, which has in recent years provided models for new ways of thinking about traditional culture as 'cultural property'. A growing literature on the controversies this has generated includes anthropologically informed accounts such as Brown 1998; Brush and Stabinsky 1996; Greaves 1994; Harrison 1992; Posey 1996.

7. The point of these excerpts is to show their international coverage; this one comes from an article syndicated from Associated Press and reproduced in part in Papua New Guinea's *Post Courier* and *The National* (both April 24 1996). It will be appreciated that I am reporting on gross stereotypes. The particular inflection which many Papua New Guineans give to 'custom' is not well served by them.

8. The NIH (National Institute of Health) Laboratory of Neurological Disorders, Washington DC, where Jenkins had had contact for some years. The virus turned out to be a variant form that had also been identified in the Solomon Islands; patenting applications for the Solomons variant were dropped, and Papua New Guinea alone was named.

9. The patent was granted to the United States of America as represented by the US Department of Health and Human Services. ['The present invention relates to a human T-cell line (PNG-1) persistently infected with a Papua New Guinea (PNG) HTLV-1 variant and to the infecting virus (PNG-1 variant)....The establishment of this cell line, the first of its kind from an individual from Papua New Guinea, makes possible the screening of Melanesian populations using a local virus.' The invention also relates to tests for the detection and diagnosis of infection using this and virus.] The patent was filed August 1992, granted March 1995, revoked October 1996; according to Cunningham (1998), the blood sample is with the American Type Culture Collection, Maryland.

10. At a meeting of the American Association of Physical Anthropologists, Jenkins apparently signed a legal paper specifying a royalty distribution, should a commercially viable product ever be developed. At one point it was reported that the distribution would be: Hagahai 50% of the total benefits, the NIH 20% and the three scientists involved in the study 10% each (*The National*, 3 October 1995).

11. They had popped up earlier in the British press in their own right, for example in the rendering in *The Times Higher Education Supplement,* 26 April 1996 ('Did the 260 Hagahai of Papua New Guinea know that their genes might offer a cure for cancer?').

12. Is the writer trying to find a commonsense connection between the media's persistent emphasis on the Hagahai's isolation and the hi-tech intrusion by suggesting that they were exposed to viruses at the same time as they were exposed to the outside world? One widely circulated story about their 'discovery' is that it was they who made contact with the outside world because they felt they were dying out and wanted western medicine. For some observers (e.g. Mangi 1988), such stories throw into doubt how 'uncontacted' these people were.

13. An expert in indigenous intellectual property rights from New Zealand, where the US patent holder was hoping to enforce the application, is quoted as saying apropos the Hagahai: 'You are taking the life blood of individuals and asserting ownership. It is bad enough that you do it to your own citizens, but much worse to do it to people of other countries.' (*The Independent* [Papua New Guinea], 1 March 1996).

14. RAFI claims to have given interviews about them to 77 different press agencies and newspapers across the world. (RAFI describes itself as an international organisation devoted to the conservation and sustainable improvement of agricultural biodiversity, and the socially responsible development of technology useful to rural societies. Its watch on genetic technologies is part of this.)

15. Used frequently in the 1995 EU debate (e.g. 'The European Parliament is expected to open the way to the patenting of human life', *The Independent* [UK], 1 March 1995).

16. And even 'human species'. Papua New Guinea's High Commissioner to New Zealand was quoted as saying, 'We have been talking about the exploitation of the environment, the rainforest, and now they are talking about the exploitation of the human species.' (*The Independent* [Papua New

Guinea], 1 March 1996). If the extrapolations seem wild, then we should consider that geneticists have protested at the very breadth of some patent applications, as for instance the patent filed to cover *all* ex vivo manipulations of malfunctioning human cells under certain conditions (*Nature*, 30 March 1995).

17. Although the man's DNA material was inevitably present in the cell line. Moreover, while the patent referred to the value of the cell line for screening and similar purposes, at the back lay potential interest in genetic factors relating to immunity. Cunningham (1998; and see Frow 1997: 152ff) provides an important amplification of these connections by putting the whole issue into the international context of the then current debate and anxiety over the Human Genome Diversity Project.

18. The Convention on Biological Diversity was an important component of the UN Conference on Environment and Development (the 'Earth Summit'), Rio 1992. It also contained other agreements, such as the Rio Declaration and 'Agenda 21', an action plan aimed at the integration of environmental concerns across a range of activities.

19. Traditionally, English common law, one of the bases of Papua New Guinea law, does not admit of property in the body (see for example the discussion in Nuffield Council on Bioethics, 1995).

20. Sengi adds that it did not take him long to realise the implications of the US patent for the Hagahai cell line patent. The parallel is made over and again.

21. And important issues they are too (see esp. Cunningham 1998 who spells out the exploitation entailed).

22. Whereas 'tribesman' is a primitivist gloss which conjures up a traditional past, the category 'tribe', like 'clan', is contemporary Papua New Guinea usage for an order of political grouping.

23. Initially they had apparently talked of two women, but only Miriam's name ever came up. At that time the Papua New Guinea kina was worth approximately £0.5 stg. For simplicity I continue to use the tribal names, although the relevant units of action were clans or sub-clans from within the tribes (Tangilka Kumu Kanem and Konumbuka Tau Kanem).

24. Muke belongs to the same Tangilka patriclan as the dead man, Willingal, and has married into the clan from which Willingal's mother had come.

25. Not that the spouse's clan take away something which the natal clan could have enjoyed for themselves (a woman must marry outside her clan). It is only when female reproductive powers are transferred in marriage that the natal clan can enjoy them, that is, when they are realised through the offspring which their woman bears for another clan. (A patrilineal paradigm for relationships is culturally appropriate for Minj.)

26. Because the wealth is carried by relationships between persons. There are situations in which persons do appear as 'things', but the details are not required here (cf. Strathern 1999).

27. They are differentiated by the directions of the flow of wealth and 'body', and thus work as reciprocals of each other.

28. Briefly, people's 'bones' (*omblom*) strengthen their paternal kin, and these payments are offered in return for that strength. In the past, making such payments was once a regular part of clan intermarriage but did not necessarily accompany death compensation. 'Head pay' was the general name given to gifts that went to the mother's kin at death.

29. Because she lived on their land, her maternal kin said they had assumed responsibility for her welfare, marriage prospects and future debt-credit relations (as a potential link person) (Muke, PNGLR 1997: 134).

30. She then went on state that she felt pressured into probably having to make a quick match, and that the payment process left her feeling lost, humiliated in the eyes of others, 'ashamed at being used as a form of payment' (PNGLR 1997: 141). One reading of her affidavit (PNGLR 1997: 141) is that it was the very fact that no-one had been named as her future spouse which made her feel she was being 'used' simply as a form of payment .

31. A substitute from the appropriate category would satisfy the criterion of a link of 'substance' – a classificatory granddaughter or someone who could stand for such a person – partly because that link is imagined in terms of the flow of (substantial) wealth which it elicits. The significant tie of descent here was from the ancestress to the men who bestowed the woman being given in marriage. O'Hanlon and Frankland (1986: 189) argue that what was at stake was less ensuring a marriage between partners already in a pre-existing relationship to one another (as anthropologists have often analysed prescriptive marriage rules between cross-cousins) than meeting a debt created by a previous marriage. The debt might or might not be tied into death compensation payments; it could be settled by a man despatching any girl whose marriage choice he controlled. However, the point about particularity remains. We may say that the woman who was given in such a way was perceived as a third generational return ('granddaughter') for a woman previously given. Whoever occupied this role, genealogical surrogate or no, occupied that role ('granddaughter') because of the specificity *of the grandmother* to whom the transaction referred. The return was not for any woman in the previous generation, but for a particular female ancestress whose identifiable progeny bore testimony to the fertility of her clan of origin.

32. But are 'marriageable men' the social analogue of 'marriageable women'? In the past, the circumstances of 'initiable men' afforded a closer parallel. (It should be noted that her kin claimed that the obligation to provide a spouse for a particular clan was different from forcing a girl onto a marriage partner, and that if she did not care for anyone, then a later marriage by someone else could always be counted retrospectively in lieu.)

33. I borrow this from UK copyright legislation (Copyright, Designs and Patent Act 1988) which recognises the moral rights of authors to be identified with their work regardless of who owns the economic rights.

34. I have not given the details, but there were a whole series of reasons to do with the fact that Miriam's grandmother had been a 'road' along which other women came to her father's clan and bore many progeny. An imbalance of persons could only be put right through altering the flow of persons.

35. For an interesting development of the concept of 'cultural specificity' see Banks 2001.

36. From Fox's (1993) history of kinship versus the state. There have been innumerable interpretations of Antigone's defiance, but he illuminates the pressure she was under as stemming from a specific and unique obligation (because of the series of tragic events) which she owed to her brother and to no-one else. She would have defied the King under no other circumstance. (I am not only talking about face-to-face relationships, although these are most evident in these examples, and in kinship contexts; but this is not the place to argue the point.)

Bibliography

Aleck, J. and J. Rannells (eds) 1995. *Custom at the Crossroads*. Port Moresby: Law Faculty, UPNG.

Banks, C. (ed.) 2001. *Developing Cultural Criminology for the Third World: Theory and Practice*. Sydney: Sydney University Press.

Banks, G. and C. Ballard (eds) 1997. *The Ok Tedi Settlement*. Canberra: Resource Management in the Asia-Pacific and National Centre for Development Studies (Pacific Policy Paper No. 27).

Barth, F. 1975. *Ritual and Knowledge amongst the Baktaman*. Oslo: Universitetsforlaget; New Haven: Yale University Press.

Barth, F. 1987. *Cosmologies in the Making: A Generative Model of Cultural Variation in Inner New Guinea*. Studies in Social Anthropology, 64. Cambridge: Cambridge University Press.

Battaglia, D. 1990. *On the Bones of the Serpent: Person, Memory and Mortality in Sabarl Island Society*. Chicago: Chicago University Press.

Bercovitch, E. 1994. 'The agent in the gift: hidden exchange in Inner New Guinea', *Cultural Anthropology* 9(4): 498–536.

Bolton, L. (ed.) 1999. *Fieldwork, Fieldworkers: Developments in Vanuatu Research*, spec. iss. *Oceania* 70(1).

Brown, M. 1998. 'Can culture be copyrighted?', *Current Anthropology* 39: 193–222.

Brush, S. and D. Stabinsky 1996. *Valuing Local Knowledge: Indigenous Peoples and Intellectual Property Rights*. Washington DC: Island Press.

Cooter, R.D. 1989. *Issues in Customary Land Law*. Discussion Paper No. 39. Port Moresby: Institute of National Affairs.

Craig, B. and D. Hyndman, (eds) 1990. *Children of Afek: Tradition and Change Among the Mountain-Ok of Central New Guinea*. Oceania Monograph 40. Sydney: University of Sydney Press.

Cronon, W. 1983. *Changes in The Land. Indians, Colonialists, and the Ecology of New England*. New York: Hill and Wang.

Crook, T. 1998. 'First Contact: What Kind of Body?', *Cambridge Anthropology* 20(1&2): 22–30.

Crook, T. 1999. 'Growing Knowledge in Bolovip, Papua New Guinea', *Oceania* 69(4): 225–42.

Crook, T. 2000. 'Length matters: a note on the GM debate', *Anthropology Today* 16(1): 8–11.

Cunningham, H. 1998. 'Colonial encounters in postcolonial contexts: patenting indigenous DNA and the Human Genome Diversity Project', *Critique of Anthropology* 18: 205–33.

Daes, E-I. 1997. *Protection of the Heritage of Indigenous People*. Geneva: Centre for Human Rights, United Nations.

de Coppet, D. 1995. ''Are'are society: a Melanesian socio-cosmic point of view: how are bigmen the servants of society and cosmos?' In de Coppet, D. and A. Iteanu, (eds) *Cosmos and Society in Oceania*. Oxford: Berg.

Englund, H. and J. Leach 2000. 'Ethnography and the meta-narratives of modernity', *Current Anthropology* 41(2): 225–48.

Ernst, T. 1999. 'Land, stories and resources: discourse and entification in Onabasulu modernity', *American Anthropologist* 101: 88–97.

Filer, C. 1993. 'Tolukuma gold mine: socio-economic impact assessment', unpublished report to Dome Resources NL and the PNG Department of Environment and Conservation.

Filer, C. 1997. 'Compensation, rent and power in Papua New Guinea.' In S. Toft (ed.) *Compensation and Resource Development*. Port Moresby: Papua New Guinea Law Reform Commission, Monograph 6; Canberra: Australian National University.

Filer, C. 1998. 'The Melanesian way of menacing the mining industry.' In L. Zimmer-Tamakoshi (ed.) *Modern Papua New Guinea*. Kirksville, MO: Thomas Jefferson University Press.

Filer, C. with N. Sekrahn 1998. *Loggers, Donors and Resource Owners: Policy that Works for Forests and People*. Port Moresby: PNG NRI; London: IIED.

Foster, R. J. 1996. *Social Reproduction and History in Melanesia: Mortuary Ritual, Gift Exchange, and Custom in the Tanga Islands*. Cambridge: Cambridge University Press.

Fox, R. 1993. *Reproduction and Succession: Studies in Anthropology, Law and Society*. New Brunswick: Transaction Publishers.

Frow, J. 1997. *Time and Commodity Culture: Essays in Cultural Theory and Postmodernity*. Oxford: Clarendon Press.

Garrity, B. 1999. 'Conflict between Maori and Western concepts of intellectual property', *Auckland University Law Review* 8: 1193–211.

Gray, K. 1987. *Elements of Land Law*. London: Butterworths.

Gewertz, D. and F. Errington 1999. *Emerging Class in Papua New Guinea: The Telling of a Difference*. Cambridge: Cambridge University Press.

Greaves, T. (ed.), 1994. *Intellectual Property Rights for Indigenous Peoples: a Sourcebook*. Oklahoma City: Society for Applied Anthropology.

Greenhouse, C. 1982. 'Looking at culture, looking for rules', *Man* (N.S.) 17, 58–73.

Haley, N. 1996. 'Polluting Desires', unpublished paper presented at the conference, *Cosmology and Development in Melanesia*, October, James Cook University, Cairns.

Hallpike, C. 1977. *Bloodshed and Vengeance in the Papuan Mountains. The Generation of Conflict in Tauade Society*. Oxford: Clarendon.

Hann, C. 1998. *Property Relations*. Cambridge: Cambridge University Press.

Harrison, S. 1992. 'Ritual as intellectual property', *Man* (N.S.) 27: 225–44.

Hirsch, E. 1987. 'Dialectics of the bowerbird: an interpretative account of ritual and symbolism in the Udabe Valley, Papua New Guinea', *Mankind* 17: 1–14.

Hirsch, E. 1994. 'Between mission and market: events and images in a Melanesian society', *Man* (N.S.) 29: 689–711.

Hirsch, E. 2001. 'New boundaries of influence in highland Papua culture, mining and ritual conversions', *Oceania* 71: 298–312.

Honore, A. M. 1961. 'Ownership.' In *Oxford Essays in Jurisprudence* (ed.) A.G. Guest. Oxford: Oxford University Press.

Ingold, T. 2000. 'Ancestry, Generation, Substance, Memory, Land.' In *The Perception of the Environment: Essays on Livelihood, Dwelling and Skill*, London: Routledge.

Jessep, O. and J. Luluaki. 1994. *Principles of Family Law in Papua New Guinea*. Waigani: University of Papua New Guinea Press.

Jorgensen, D. 1996. 'Regional history and ethnic identity in the hub of New Guinea: the emergence of the Min', *Oceania*, 66(3): 189–210.

Jorgensen, D. n.d.a 'Generic tradition, legibility and the politics of identity in a Papua New Guinea mining project', paper for session "Inequality, the state and the meanings of 'tradition': cases from Southeast Asia and Melanesia", AAA, November 1999).

Jorgenson, D. n.d.b 'The conquest of Nena: property, identity and the politics of mining in Papua New Guinea', unpublished paper.

Josephides, L. 1985. *The Production Of Inequality: Gender And Exchange Among The Kewa*. London: Tavistock.

Kalinoe, L. 1993. 'Determining ownership of customary land in Papua New Guinea: Re Hides gas land project case', *Melanesian Law Journal* 21: 1–12.

Kalinoe, L. 1999. *Water Law and Customary Water Rights in Papua New Guinea*. New Delhi: UBS Publishers Distributors Ltd.

Kalinoe, L. n.d. 'Accessing indigenous intellectual and cultural property or traditional knowledge in Papua New Guinea: Legal Options', paper presented to PTC Workshop 5, Cambridge, March 2000.

Kalinoe, L. and Kuwimb, J. 1996. 'Natural resource law and policy in Papua New Guinea', *Australasian Journal of Natural Resources Law and Policy* 3(1): 147–72.

Kalinoe, L. and J. Simet 1999. 'Cultural policy to oversee management of cultures, cultural material', *The Independent* [PNG], 23 September 1999; see also in *Symposium on Protection Of Traditional Knowledge and Expression of Indigenous Cultures in the Pacific Islands*, 1999, Noumea: UNESCO and South Pacific Commission.

Kirsch, S. 1997a. 'Lost tribes: Indigenous people and the social imaginary', *Anthropological Quarterly* 70: 58–67.

Kirsch, S. 1997b. 'Indigenous response to environmental impact along the Ok Tedi River.' In *Compensation For Resource Development In Papua New Guinea*, (ed.) S. Toft. Port Moresby and Canberra: Law Reform Commission Monograph No. 6, Resource Management in Asia-Pacific, and National Centre for Development Studies, Pacific Policy Paper 24, 143–155.

Knauft, B. 1999. *From Primitive to Postcolonial in Melanesia and Anthropology*. Ann Arbor: University of Michigan Press.

Latour, B. 1993. *We Have Never Been Modern*. (tr.) Catherine Porter. Cambridge, MA: Harvard University Press.

Law Reform Commission 1977. *The Role of Customary Law in the Legal System*. Waigani: Law Reform Commission Report No. 7.

Lawrence, P. 1969. 'The state versus stateless societies in Papua and New Guinea.' In *Fashion of Law in New Guinea* (ed.) B.J. Brown. Sydney: Butterworths.

Lawrence, P. 1984. *The Garia. An Ethnography of a Traditional Cosmic System in Papua New Guinea*. Carlton: Melbourne University Press.

Lea, D. 1994. 'Lockean property rights, Tully's community ownership, and Melanesian customary communal ownership', *Journal of Social Philosophy* 25(1): 117.

Leach, J. 2000. 'Situated connections: rights and intellectual resources in a Rai Coast (PNG) society', *Social Anthropology* 8(2): 163–79.

Leach, J. 2002. 'Drum and voice. Aesthetics and social process on the Rai Coast of Papua New Guinea', *Journal of the Royal Anthropological Institute* (N.S.) 8: 713–34.

MacIntyre, A. 1999. *Dependent Rational Animals*. London: Duckworth.

Macintyre, M. n.d. 'Substitutions and transformations in exchange systems in the context of economic change: gifts and money on Tubetube and Lihir', unpublished paper.

Mangi, J. 1988. 'On the question of the "lost tribes": a report on a field trip of 24–30 April 1984', University of Papua New Guinea Schrader Mountains Report No. 4, *Research in Melanesia* 9 : 37–65.

Mosko, M. 1983. 'Conception, de-conception and social structure in Bush Mekeo Culture.' In *Concepts of Conception*, ed. D. Jorgensen, spec. issue, *Mankind* 14.

Munn, N. 1990. 'Constructing regional worlds in experience: Kula exchange, witchcraft and Gawan local events', *Man* (N.S.) 25, 1–17.

Muke, J. n.d. 'The case of the compo girl: kinship on trial', paper presented to Dept. of Social Anthropology. Cambridge 1996.

Narakobi, B. 1982. 'History and movement in law reform in Papua New Guinea.' In D. Weisbrot, A. Pailiwala and A. Sawyers (eds), *Law and Social Change in Papua New Guinea*. Sydney: Butterworths.

Nuffield Council on Bioethics. 1995. *Human Tissue: Ethical and Legal Issues*. London: Nuffield Council on Bioethics.

O'Hanlon, M. and L. Frankland 1986. 'With a skull in the netbag: prescriptive marriage and matrilateral relations in the New Guinea Highlands', *Oceania* 56: 181–98.

Paliwala, A. 1982. 'Law and order in the village: The village courts.' In D. Weisbrot, A. Paliwala and A. Sawyerr (eds) *Law and Social Change in Papua New Guinea*. Sydney: Butterworths.

PNGLR 1997. 'In the matter of an application under Section 57 of the Constitution: application by Individual and Community Rights Forum Inc. (ICRAF) in re: Miriam Willingal, National Court of Justice', *Papua New Guinea Law Reports,* Port Moresby.

Pottage, A. 1998. 'The inscription of life in law: genes, parents, and bio-politics', *Modern Law Review* 61: 740–65.

Posey, D. 1996. *Traditional Resource Rights: International instruments for Protection and Compensation for Indigenous Peoples and Local Communities*. Gland, Switzerland, and Cambridge: International Union for Conservation of Nature.

Posey, D. and G. Dutfield 1996. *Beyond Intellectual Property: Toward Traditional Resource Rights for Indigenous Peoples and Local Communities*. Ottawa: International Development Research Centre.

Rabinow, P. 1996. *Essays on the Anthropology of Reason*. Princeton: Princeton University Press.

Radin, M. 1996. *Contested Commodities: The Trouble with Trade in Sex, Children, Body Parts, and Other Things*. Cambridge, Mass.: Harvard University Press.

Riles, A. 1994. 'Representing in-between: Law, anthropology, and the rhetoric of interdisciplinarity', *University of Illinois Law Review* 3, 597–650.

Riles, A. 1998. 'Infinity within the brackets', *American Ethnologist* 25(3): 378–98.

Riles, A. (ed.) n.d. *Documents: Artefacts of Modern Knowledge*, Durham, N.C: Duke University Press.

Rose, C. 1994. *Property as Persuasion: Essays on the History Theory, and Rhetoric of Ownership*. Boulder, CO: Westview.

Rumsey, A. 2000. 'Agency, personhood and the 'I' of discourse in the Pacific and beyond', *The Journal of the Royal Anthropological Institute* 6: 101–15.

Salisbury, R. 1988. 'The Miyamiya group of peoples, 16–17 February 1984', University of Papua New Guinea Schrader Mountains Report No. 1, *Research in Melanesia* 9 : 6–24.

Scaglion, R. 1990. 'Legal adaptation in a Papua New Guinea village court', *Ethnology* 29: 17–33.

Stewart, W. J. and Burgess, R. 1996 *Collins Dictionary of Law*. Glasgow: Harper-Collins Publishers.

Strathern, M. 1972. *Women in Between: Female Roles in a Male World*. London: Seminar [Academic] Press.

Strathern, M. 1988. *The Gender of The Gift. Problems with Women and Problems with Society in Melanesia*. Berkeley: University of California Press.

Strathern, M. 1996. 'Cutting the Network', *Journal of the Royal Anthropological Institute* 2(3): 517-35.

Strathern, M. 1998a. 'Divisions of interests and languages of ownership.' In C.M. Hann (ed.) *Property Relations*. Cambridge: Cambridge University Press.

Strathern, M. 1998b. 'The new modernities.' In V. Keck (ed.) *Common Worlds and Single Lives: Constituting Knowledge in Pacific Societies*. Oxford: Berg.

Strathern, M. 1999. *Property, Substance and Effect. Anthropological Essays on Persons and Things*. London: Athlone.

Strathern, M. 2001. 'The patent and the Malanggan', *Theory, Culture & Society 18(4): 1–26.*

Sturzenhofecker, G. 1994. 'Visions of a landscape. Duna pre-meditations on ecological change', *Canberra Anthropology* 17: 27–47.

Swanson, T. (ed.) 1995. *Intellectual Property Right and Biodiversity Conservation: An Interdisciplinary Analysis of the Values of Medicinal Plants*. Cambridge University Press.

Sykes, K. with conclusions by J. Simet 2000. *Cultural Property in the New Guinea Island Region*. New Delhi: UBS Publishers' Distributors Ltd.

Titmuss, R. 1997. [1970] *The Gift Relationship: From Human Blood to Social Policy*. Original edition with new chapters, (ed.) by A. Oakley and J. Ashton, London: LSE Books.

Thompson, [no initial] 2000. 'Investigation of Pig Mortalities Lihir Island, 20–23 January 2000: Preliminary Report', unpublished report.

Toft, S. 1997. (ed.) *Compensation and Resource Development in Papua New Guinea*. Canberra: Australian National University; Port Moresby: Law Reform Commission.

Turner, J. W. C. 1941. 'Some Reflections on Ownership in English Law', *Canadian Bar Review* 343.

Tyler, E. L. G. and N. E. Palmer 1973. *Personal Property*. London: Butterworths.

van Baal, J. 1966. *Dema: Description and Analysis of Marind-anim Culture (South New Guinea)*. The Hague: Martinus Nijhoff.

Wagner, R. 1967. *The Curse of Souw*. Chicago: Chicago University Press.

Wagner, R. 1974. 'Are there social groups in the New Guinea Highlands.' In M.J. Leaf (ed.) *Frontiers of Anthropology*. New York: D van Nostrand Company.

Weiner, J. 1986. *The Heart of the Pearlshell: The Mythological dimension of Foi Sociality*. Berkeley: California University Press.

Weiner, J. 1995. *The Lost Drum. The Myth of Sexuality in Papua New Guinea and Beyond*. Madison, WI: University of Wisconsin Press.

Weiner, J. 1998. 'The incorporated ground: the contemporary work of distribution in the Kutubu oil project area, Papua New Guinea', *Resource Management in Asia-Pacific Working Paper* No. 17. Research School for Pacific and Asian Studies, Australian National University: Canberra.

Westermark, G.D. 1986. 'Court is an arrow: legal pluralism in Papua New Guinea', *Ethnology* 25, 131–49.

Williamson, H. 1989. Conflicting Claims to the Gardens of the Sea: the Traditional Ownership of Resources in the Trobriand Islands of Papua New Guinea *Melanesian Law Journal* 17: 26.

Williamson, R. 1912. *The Mafulu Mountain People of British New Guinea*. London: Macmillan.

Young, M. 1974. 'Private sanctions and public ideology: Some aspects of self-help in Kalauna, Goodenough Island.' In A.L. Epstein (ed.) *Contention and Dispute: Aspects of Law and Social Control in Melanesia*. Canberra: Australian National University Press.

Matrix of Issues Arising from the Cases

Each chapter has been written to provide specific and concrete instances of people's expectations about ownership. In the specific cases are also issues of general significance; several of these converge, that is, the same or similar issues crop up in different contexts. We focus here on the role which people accord their relations with one another. Reference is by chapter number (2–8).

Values Expressed in the Acting Out of Social Relations

1. Relationships are in themselves a source of value

Although disputes and claims may concern goods (things) or land, in many cases it is the value that ongoing relationships have for people which surfaces as the object of concern. They may be quite explicit about this (e.g. 7). So there are examples of disputants dropping claims in order to avoid severing productive relations (4), processes by which people measure relations with one another through exchange (6), and a recognition that conflicts which harm persons, and thus are directly about their relations with others, are qualitatively different from conflicts over (say) land title (3). All this has an abstract side: past relationships are rehearsed in the present; these may be recalled through the recitation of genealogy (5), or as part of the specific knowledge an individual has acquired, given as a series of names (2). Relations here can be between individual persons or between groups (8).

2. Transactions (between two or more parties) create their own histories

The issue here is not so much the sustaining of general relations, between persons or between groups, but the careers or particular histories of interactions. Whether or not they are formalised into sets of exchanges between exchange partners, the purchase, exchange or transfer of tangible (wealth, food) and intangible items (magic, knowledge) creates a history of debts and obligations. Like interactions between kin or spouses over a period (3), this can be seen in respect of rights to land (4), in caring for kin (7), in the chain of events that are spread out in compensation claims (6), and in the way previous transactions lie behind present ones (8). This may modify the *exercise* of ownership claims (5). Relevant transactions (e.g. a purchase, 2) may also be located in the past.

3. It is characteristic of enduring relations that a dispute over one thing may also be a dispute over another

Although it is a commonplace that disputes (as a series of interactions) always have a history to them, these chapters point to something else: that people may deliberately use one example to think about another (7). We see this in two cases involving the cutting of trees: one (3) revived old jealousies about access to outside resources, while the other (4) recalled past land disputes when what was wanted was a share in the profits. In further cases, a particular marriage arrangement (8) turned out to be about an long-standing imbalance between groups, and (2) a new representation of land boundaries appeared by way of analogy to the kind of land claims stimulated by mining ventures. Enduring relations of this kind are found in the network of ties between a mining company and local communities (6).

4. Tangible and intangible things stand for one another as evidence about the quality of relations

That land, or water courses (5), can be made productive through work may be taken as a sign of the state of people's relationships with one another or with ancestors or spirits. People look for 'signs' about the state of relationships (3, 7). They also look for 'signs' of changes in the productive relations between persons (4) – so that 'ownership' claims may emerge in prospect of new assets, especially when they come through the road of 'development' (also 2, 6, 8).

5. Persons are not isolates; groups are not isolates

A person's dependency on group membership for access to certain resources may be anticipated or be manifest (2, 5). However, there may well be a difference between men and women in the way attachment can be exercised, so the nature of the dependencies will be different (8). People are often quite explicit about domestic dependencies, inherent to interaction between spouses (3), and kin relations of all kinds. At the same time, men in particular emphasise the way in which groups depend on one another, inherent in the very notion of intermarriage between clans (4) and ideas about divisions between maternal and paternal kin (7) , as well as in the activation of extensive networks (6).

Summary Index

List of Examples, Disputes and Court Cases Dealing with Ownership and Related Matters

Chapter 2 (Fuyuge, Central Province)

An ethnographic example: Comparison of land narratives between mid-1980s and 1999 shows, in both cases, how claims are established through types of personal knowledge. However, the implications of allowing other people to live on one's land had changed in the context of people's expectations about the imminent Tolukuma gold mine. Expanded versions of ongoing land narratives appeared to take on the idea of clear boundaries that could be 'mapped' onto the ground; current ownership claims had to be made persuasive.

Chapter 3 (Suau, Milne Bay Province)

1. Village Court, 1999: The case involved the destruction of a house in the violent aftermath of misunderstandings between affines over a bridewealth return. Compensation was ruled: 100K to rebuild the house and a pig out of respect for its owner – relations have a future when transactions keep the channels open.

2. Village Court, 1999: Deliberated the consequences of wife-beating in context of deteriorating relations. On learning that she did not want to leave her husband, the magistrates ordered him to provide the resources for a feast for the wife; other parties were fined by the court for inciting her.

3. Informal 'court', 2000: A land mediation. Two trees were cut when permission had been given for one. Question between cross-cousins of who had the right to determine the use. The matter was thoroughly aired, and ended with a promise of no further felling; no compensation paid (the transaction would have made the cross-cousins like affines – here implying undesirable differentiation).

Chapter 4 (Nekgini, Madang Province)

1. Informal confrontation, 1988: Road building leads to encroachment on land of another group and to recall of earlier grants of land which had been gifted along with *kastom* knowledge and designs. Threatened with the return of the *kastom*, complainants withdraw for fear of cutting off the sharing of resources and productive relations generally between them.

2. Informal dispute resolution, 1995: Cutting timber for a slit-gong drum intended for purchase revives a former land dispute (case 1). No-one wants the timber (or land) back – complainants want a share of 'profits' now the land is newly productive ('development'), but again withdraw under threat of disengagement of all relations between the two sides and dissolution of *kastom* cooperation.

Chapter 5 (Common law and national laws, PNG)

1. Land Titles Commission, 1993 [Re Hides Gas Project Land Case [1993] PNGLR 309]: A disagreement between clans both claiming land through extensive genealogies and local knowledge led to a judgement which ignored traditional knowledge altogether. The judge ruled in favour of the clan which had possession (occupied the land). This converts 'possesson' into 'ownership', and obscures the relationship between the parties.

Other citations:
2. Administration of Papua New Guinea v Guba Doriga [1973] ALJR 621
3. Re Fishermen Island Case [1979] PNGLR 202
4. Madana Resena v Papua New Guinea [1990] PNGLR
5. The Tubantia [1924]
6. Young v Hichens [1834] 6 Q.B. 606
7. Mabo (No 2) [1992] 107 ALR 1
8. State v Giddings [1981] PNGLR 423

Chapter 6 (Lihir, New Ireland)

1. Direct claim and settlement, 1999: Compensation was demanded from Lihir gold mine for the death of pigs allegedly caused by pollution, and was settled by the mining company. This leads to a further demand: company responds by determining the cause of death in their eyes but pays compensation for general loss of resources, while Lihir people see relations caught up in a long chain of events.

2. Ongoing settlements, Current: The mining company regularly meets villager demands for compensation for pigs killed in accidents on the road it built. The rationales cover attributions and denials of responsibility in relation to the road itself and to the drivers of vehicles.

3. An Ethnographic example: Old and new currencies in transactions. The way in which people produce pigs from cash incorporates cash into inter-clan exchanges so as to maximise prestige. At the same time, such exchange stimulates the production of shells used both as a regular form of currency and as valuables.

Chapter 7 (Angkaiyakmin people, Bolivip, Western Province 1994–9)

1. An ethnographic example: The transmission of knowledge. Principles in transmission of *awem* (important knowledge) from seniors to juniors is ideally the combination of two sources from two different sets of kin, like the combination of maternal and paternal substance in the creation of children. The logic of 'two sides' is followed through several instances.

2. An ethnographic example: Mortuary payments. The man's side and woman's side are separated at a death by the one giving valuables to (and receiving from) the other.

Expressions of anger lead to violence against persons and property (cf. Chapter 3, case 1). Kinship-based obligations are cross-cut by rationales to do with recent history of interpersonal relations and residence.

Chapter 8 (National and international arenas)

1. International debate, 1995–7: The 'Hagahai blood saga'. A Canadian human rights group compels the USA to rescind a patent on products from a Hagahai (Madang Province) man's blood . One of the arguments was that no compensation had been forthcoming. No law suit, but informal international pressure.

2. National Court, Mt Hagen, 1997 [In the matter of an application under Section 57 of the Constitution: application by Individual and Community Rights Forum Inc. (ICRAF) in re: Miriam Willingal, PNGLR 1997]. A NGO human rights group in PNG takes two Minj tribes to court for including a woman in a compensation payment. The logic is similar to that of the mortuary payments recorded in Chapter 7, example 1. The judge rules that including a woman is contrary to the Constitution and the groups are ordered to desist from customary practices.

Also available from
Sean Kingston Publishing

Commons and Borderlands
Working Papers on Interdisciplinarity, Accountability and the Flow of Knowledge
Marilyn Strathern

In *Commons and Borderlands* a leading social anthropologist examines early twenty-first-century interests in interdisciplinarity, with particular attention to the conjunction of science and society. Interdisciplinary practice has become well entrenched in any number of scientific disciplines, or disciplines from the humanities or from social science for that matter. This does not deter current rhetoric which sees new opportunities in new combinations of interests. One arresting strand is the promise that in a strong form – transdisciplinarity – 'science' might thereby be brought into 'society'. Marilyn Strathern's questioning of this process addresses the challenge that notions of property ownership pose to the expected flow of knowledge. As is fitting for a consideration of the flow and transformational properties of knowledge, the contents of this collection are knowingly designated 'working papers', left as open, unfinished statements to highlight their future and the work they may still do. They are designed to inspire debate, and publication will coincide with a Cambridge seminar series on Social Property at which many of these challenges will be rehearsed and articulated.

Marilyn Strathern is William Wyse Professor of Social Anthropology, University of Cambridge.
Paperback: ISBN 0-9545572-2-0 £12.99 / $20.99;
Available February 2004

Mining and Indigenous Lifeworlds in Australia and Papua New Guinea
Edited by *Alan Rumsey* and *James Weiner*

'The writing is new and interesting. The essays mark out new ideas in seemingly effortless abundance… In sum – buy it, read it, I think you'll agree that it's one of the really interesting books of the year.' (**Deborah Rose**, Senior Fellow, Centre for Resource and Environmental Studies, ANU)

order online at
WWW.SEANKINGSTON.CO.UK

Printed in the United Kingdom
by Lightning Source UK Ltd.
121108UK00002B/89